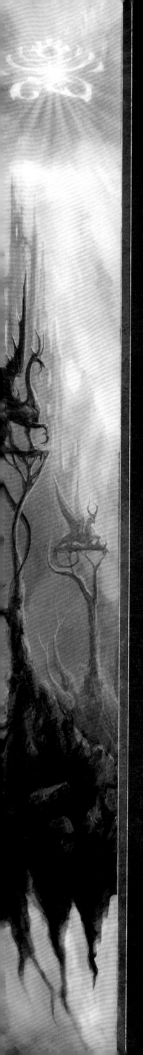

The Realm-lords, the Lumineth call themselves, for their mastery over the lands is unrivalled.

These numinous beings, the aelven scions of the twin gods Tyrion and Teclis, have scintillating magic in their blood. They have dwelt long in Hysh, the Realm of Light, where enlightenment and skill saturates the very air. The Lumineth have absorbed so much of this innate potential that, when at war, they glow with lambent power. To face their warhosts in battle is to face a barrage of magic, a forest of blades, a crashing assault of elemental wrath.

That claim of mastery also carries a deadly arrogance. The Lumineth come in glory, but they hail from a broken land, their elegant spires toppled and their statuary crumbled in the dust of a dead empire. The stories tell that it was the scourge of Chaos that ravaged Hysh, that the transformation of the Ten Paradises into spell-haunted ruin was unavoidable, but it was a terrible civil war that opened the door.

Since the time of the Reinvention, the Lumineth have made their peace with the lands they call home. Now they go to war in all the splendour of bygone days, the warrior Vanari phalanxes gleaming bright, catching the blinding rays of magic sent searing out by the gifted Scinari caste. Alongside them march the warriors of the aelementiri temples, those who have bonded in mind, body and spirit with the geomantic entities of their shattered homelands. Most majestic of all are the towering avatars of those magical places, the war forms of Hysh itself. All those who threaten the Lumineth's agenda will be mercilessly removed from existence.

The Lumineth fight a war for reality itself, and in that war, there can be no sacrifice too great...

CONTENTS

2

PRODUCED BY THE WARHAMMER STUDIO
With thanks to The Faithful for their additional playtesting services.

Order Battletome: Lumineth Realm-lords © Copyright Games Workshop Limited 2020. Order Battletome: Lumineth Realm-lords, GW, Games Workshop, Warhammer, Stormcast Eternals, and all associated logos, illustrations, images, names, creatures, races, vehicles, locations, weapons, characters, and the distinctive likenesses thereof, are either ® or TM, and/or © Games Workshop Limited, variably registered around the world. All Rights Reserved.

Games Workshop Ltd., Willow Road, Lenton, Nottingham, NG7 2WS, United Kingdom
games-workshop.com

Archmage Teclis leads the Lumineth host to war, the brilliant light of Hysh heralding a spectacular display of magic and dazzling skill that sends the enemy reeling.

THE AELVES OF HYSH

The Lumineth are often mistaken for angelic beings of pure light, for they glow with the glorious power of Hysh. Their incredible intellects were once turned to the pursuits of art, magic and philosophy, but now they are attuned to the business of war. To fight them is to battle not only the aelven warhosts but the Realm of Light itself.

Graceful of mind as well as of body, the Lumineth Realm-lords are the quintessence of all that is aelven. Their speech is eloquent and their mastery of arcane matters supreme, for the Ten Paradises of Hysh have blessed them with uncanny intellect. The Lumineth consider themselves the most advanced of all living creatures, and they would gladly devote their entire existence to the furtherance of their own fields of expertise. But since the disasters of the Age of Chaos, they have recognised the need to take up arms in defence of the Mortal Realms, lest the cosmos be torn to shreds by the Dark Gods.

In battle, the Realm-lords fight with impressive precision. Each pinpoint thrust of the blade, each weaving evasion, each step and stride is executed with the poise and confidence of a master fencer. Their spells are crafted with expert skill, beams of light and darts of pure energy searing out to strike with unerring accuracy, for to the Lumineth, a spell is not a weapon but an art form. It is not rage or battle-lust that drives the aelves of Hysh to such lethality but painstaking, logical analysis.

Only now, as the Age of Sigmar takes hold, is the true power of the Hyshian aelves becoming clear. Sent to war by Archmage Teclis and his brother Tyrion, the Lord of Lumination, they fight to change history with each new battle. Where once they fought as individuals, they now do so as superbly disciplined phalanxes of warriors. Their archers and mages work in concert, harrying the foe from afar with blistering magic and expert marksmanship before their pike-wielding kin impale the survivors on the white-hot tips of their blades. Those who prove strong or numerous enough to endure against the rank and file are ridden down by elite cavalry mounted on sleek chargers or smashed to pieces by the aelementiri disciples of the Hyshian temples and their war-spirit allies.

The Lumineth have a dark history, falling from the light into darkness of their own creation. They came back from the brink, however, and in doing so found themselves able to see flaws that had remained hidden even under the ever-present light of Hysh. Since the time of atonement known as the Reinvention, the Lumineth have made peace with the lands they call home. Yet there still remains a kernel of hubris that they cannot acknowledge – or perhaps cannot even see. Truly, it is said that the Lumineth see furthest of all, yet they are blinded by their own brilliance, for though they are quick to judge those they see as inferior, all too often they cannot perceive the flaws in their own diamond-bright souls.

The Lumineth have long shunned emotion, for the prevailing opinion is that it clouds the mind and detracts from the perfection of pure thought. Worse still, powerful emotion may lead to the incarnation of echoes in the aether, as exemplified by Slaanesh's daemons and the forbidden works of aelven scholars who have dabbled in summonation. They believe that a soul inflamed by anger will act hastily, even rashly, just as one in thrall to compassion might act in a fashion that saves one life but endangers many more.

Given their aloof and inscrutable manner, the Hyshian aelves have made many enemies, even in times of peace. For long millennia, the Lumineth fought only for their secluded homelands, since they believed all the other realms to be poor cousins by comparison. In the wider realms, the aelves of Hysh have a reputation as a deadly and unpredictable race, for should they deem a particular settlement to be standing in the way of their wider goals, they will obliterate it with neither hesitation nor explanation.

The very detachment that the Lumineth prize was once proven to be a grave weakness. To devalue emotion to the point of burying it altogether is to invite disaster, as shown by the great cataclysm of the Spirefall that marked the dawn of the Age of Chaos in Hysh. The repression of the Lumineth's true desires flared up into spiteful feelings, then sabotage, then open violence. This was no usual civil war; it was a magical apocalypse that ravaged every one of the Ten Paradises and tore down much of the glorious empire the aelves had built.

Since then, the Lumineth have been forced to radically change their outlook and the way they use the resources of Hysh, the magical realmstone known as aetherquartz in particular. They have recently achieved symbiosis with the realm, working in concert with it rather than seeking to transcend it as they did throughout the Age of Myth. Led in this new direction by Lord Teclis, master of the arcane, the Lumineth go to war alongside the avatars of the Realm of Light itself. By uniting with the power of Hysh, the Lumineth war machine has been invigorated. Now, with the elemental manifestations of river, mountain, wind and zenith in league with them – and even fighting alongside them in their war forms – they are more dangerous than ever.

THE HYSHIAN WARHOSTS

The armies of the Lumineth are formed largely of citizen warriors. Each of the aelves that forms their military has a rich and fulfilling life outside the call of battle; indeed, were it not for the dire state of the realms and the omnipresent threat of Chaos, it is likely they would not go to war at all. The vast majority of the Lumineth prefer to spend their time in pursuits of the mind and soul rather than of the body, and physical conflict has always been seen as rather brutish and unrefined in the high society of the aelves.

Since the passing of the Decree Tyrionic, a dictat laid down at the dawn of the Age of Sigmar, each of Hysh's nations maintains a standing army of Vanari, a warhost with exhaustive training in military theory, led by the Scinari mage caste. They seek to twin the magic of the spirit with the excellence of the body, just as the gods Teclis and Tyrion reflect two sides of the same soul. The elemental principles of the Hyshian moons are coupled with those of the symbolic sun to provide a greater form of illumination than either taken in isolation. In this is the key to a truly balanced soul.

Realising that the fate of the Mortal Realms hangs in the balance, the aelves of Hysh have struck out into the war for reality itself. With foresight and skill, the Lumineth have systematically pushed back the Chaos invaders from many of the corrupted regions of the Ten Paradises. Buoyed by their victories thus far, they have journeyed through dozens of Realmgates in order to bring their wisdom to the other Mortal Realms. In the wake of each victory, the Lumineth use geomantic magic to purify the lands, performing arcane rites to engrave vast symbols across them and thereby ensure they are rendered stable for the betterment of all. To the Realm-lords, whether or not this requires the decimation of their allies' territory is immaterial.

Perhaps in overruling and alienating those who would fight for the same cause, they have already overreached themselves. After all, Chaos – and particularly their nemesis Slaanesh – is a force that thrives on strife, no matter its provenance.

THE REALM OF LIGHT

The Realm of Light appears as a bright sun in the skies of all other realms, illuminating the cosmos until it is eclipsed by the darkness of its twin realm, Ulgu. Both pure light and the essence of enlightenment emanate from Hysh. In other realms, it can be felt as a glow within the mind as well as upon the skin; it can be healing, in its own fashion, and brings a purity of thought that can inspire even a witless dullard. Those who hail from Hysh are usually intelligent and quick of thought, but those who climb to the highest mental states of existence may find they regret their ambition a little too late. For that same light, so wondrous in capacity, can blind and bewilder, melting the minds of those who look too long upon it. Those who become besotted with the light of Hysh will find only obsession, addiction and, ultimately, annihilation. To find the balance between harnessing that power and remaining pure of soul is the ultimate goal of all true Lumineth.

Narquellian of Mithris leapt high, lancing his blade through the last of the flying daemons. The human leader stared up at him in awe. His greasy moustache quivered as he searched for the right words. Narquellian fought back his disgust. To purposefully grow hair around one's mouth… it beggared belief. But now was not the time. The portal in the city sprawling below had to be closed – and soon.

'Note the classic Dawnrider encirclement,' said Narquellian, his finger sketching envelopments in the air that bracketed the glowing rift in the abattoir.

'So… the city is saved?' said the burgomeister.

'Victory has many meanings,' said Narquellian.

'Right, but we have them surrounded in the jewellery quarter, and you aelves have the butchers' district sewn up. The day is won. The city is saved.'

Narquellian felt his eyelid twitch. He had taken a daemon's claw to the chest that morning, and it had pierced his lung. Even breathing was painful. But he would not show weakness. He would inspire, as ever.

'There is victory, and there is victory. The portal must be sealed. Cauterised.' He motioned to his Scinari, and as one they began the rite of banishment.

The hideous red wound in reality that pulsed in the dirty human city began to shrink. Bright Scinari runes arced in the twilight air, circling the portal like satellite bodies orbiting a realmsphere. The Vanari infantry, penning in the vile daemon creatures that had once butchered the human citizens, were a ring of burning blades and glimmering arrows that drove the hateful creatures back into the hell-realm one by one.

'Avert your eyes,' said Narquellian. He raised his sword and gave the signal to complete the great work.

Lines of white fire burned through the districts, scything across the urban sprawl to leave only smoking ruin. Screams rose anew as hundreds of citizens died, but Elui, a mile-wide symbol of denial, was complete.

'Madman!' sputtered the human leader, his eyes bulging. He drew his dagger, but Narquellian was already in motion, his sword's pommel striking the human on the temple so hard it knocked him out cold.

'Put him with the rest,' said the aelf. 'Duty calls.'

Like the sun they burn, brilliant and blinding. Like the river they run, flowing around all resistance. At need, they stand implacable, the strength of the mountain carried with them. They are swift as the wind; their magic is the zenith of arcane artifice. They are the Lumineth, and even the Dark Prince Slaanesh has learnt to fear them.

THE AGE OF MYTH

The origins of the Lumineth Realm-lords' empire harks back to the first days of the Mortal Realms, when Tyrion and Teclis roamed the Ten Paradises but found none of their kindred. Since that time, they have chained a god, rescued the lost souls of their fellows and created an entirely new race that raised its spires of intellect to the sky.

Towards the end of the Age of Myth, an alliance of light and shadow saw Tyrion, Teclis, Malerion and Morathi work together to entrap the nemesis of the aelves, Slaanesh. Yet before that great victory – and the crushing, self-inflicted defeat that followed it – there occurred a string of great deeds and strange adventures. These have become legend amongst the Lumineth, blurred by the passage of long centuries until dream and reality, truth and fable blended into one.

The story goes that the god Tyrion awakened in Xintil, at the heart of Hysh, after the devastating demise of the world-that-was. Having being soul-bound with the Wind of Hysh in his former existence, Tyrion had absorbed much of its power, and though his last days spent in the World Before Time had been troubled indeed, he had been reborn as a phoenix from the flames. His mortal frailties were long gone; to all intents and purposes, he had become a god of light and brilliance.

Long and lonely did Tyrion wander across the Ten Paradises, marvelling at one glorious sight after another but with a great sense of disquiet that he was alone – a hollow feeling in the soul that only a twin bereft of their sibling could hope to understand. Here was a domain he had only glimpsed in dreams, a realm that was unfolding its secrets before him, league by league. Just by being there, he felt his mind sharpen and come into focus.

As he roamed the Ten Paradises, he took in every detail, reading much into the symbolism and symmetry of the landscapes stretching before him. Again, he felt a pang of loss, for he knew his brother would have thrilled to see such geomantic splendour. At times, when he concentrated hardest, he thought he could hear his brother's voice upon the wind. It urged him onward, pushing him to

travel further away from the heart of Hysh and on towards the Realm's Edge. The lands he encountered became ever more exotic, the beams of magical light in the sky lancing into his eyes and causing his vision to fill with kaleidoscopic shards of meaning. Still he travelled, his sword laying low every eldritch beast that took him for prey, his brother's voice spurring him on from the back of his mind. Fear of the unknown was pointless for one who had died and been reborn a god, and distance had lost all meaning.

After crossing the Luminaris Sea, that body of liquid light that girdles the edge of the realm, Tyrion came to Haixiah. There, many of the lands were geometrically perfect. Their plains were as level and flawless as mirrors and their fjords were fractal-edged, their shapes repeating even at the tiniest level. The closer to the Realm's Edge he roamed, the more reality faded; washed out by the sheer intensity of the light that shone there, it became little more than a pencil sketch, then a cluster of dots, then nothing more than a concept or wave of thought. Still Tyrion pushed onwards, heedless of the dangers ahead.

It was too much, even for him. Though he ventured miles further than any mortal could have done and uncovered many revelations

about the nature of mind, body and spirit, he stared at the raw light of Hysh for so long that his eyes melted within his skull. Yet in doing so, he piqued the curiosity of the Realm's Edge itself – the elemental spirit of brilliant light that occupied the Perimeter Inimical and shone as the blazing sun across all the realms. It appeared to Tyrion in all its blinding splendour, but as the Lord of Lumination had already lost his eyes, he did not look away. There, aelf and spirit found common cause. Tyrion remembers nothing of the encounter, but he awoke once more at the realm's heart. There, lying next to him, was the recumbent body of his brother Teclis – still weak of limb as he had been since birth but with a lambent glow pouring out of him. The two had become twin halves of the same godly power, which, instead of being divided or lessened, became reflected and magnified. Tyrion found that he could see through the eyes of his brother, and, over time, Teclis taught him to assess the realms around him through extra-sensory perception. Together, they walked the lands of Hysh as gods.

Tyrion and Teclis wandered the Ten Paradises for many years, looking high and low for their kin. To their bottomless disappointment, they found not a soul. There was no remnant of the World Before Time in this new and scintillating land; for all its glory, it was strange and foreign – even to Tyrion, who had roamed far and wide before losing his sight. It was not until the twin gods found the God-King Sigmar that they encountered an echo of the world-that-was. Glad was that greeting, with much laughter and rejoicing. Here were three god-like beings with a fresh chance at creating an existence free from the taint of the Chaos Gods.

The gods made common cause swiftly, for they would all see order and justice rise anew, and they took joy in their limitless potential. Yet that joy turned to sadness when Sigmar confirmed that he had encountered scant few aelven souls as he had fanned the flames of civilisation across each of the Mortal Realms – and with those few gladly seeking refuge in Azyrheim, there were likely no more to be found. The vast majority of their race had been consumed by Slaanesh.

Reluctant to admit the truth, and readier to trust their own far-scrying vision than that of a god they had long considered a barbarian, the twin deities broadened their search. In deepest Haixiah, they climbed the highest dune in the Desert of Ending, the shimmering heat haze at its crest a portal to Shyish, for they reasoned that if their kith and kin were dead, they may have emerged in an aelven underworld. They descended the other side into the Realm of Death, but after years of searching, found nothing. To their dismay, their lost kin were absent even there.

However, their search was not entirely fruitless. In Shyish, they found a group of strange monks who informed them that a being known as Malerion also sought the souls of the lost aelves. Malerion was of Ulgu just as the twin gods were of Hysh, and just as they could not venture into the Shadow Realm, he could not step into the Realm of Light. But here, in Shyish, they could co-exist. Teclis recognised his description as an old compatriot from the world-that-was, and, with a mixture of hope and trepidation, he and his brother followed the monks to Malerion's location. There, as the reincarnated aelven gods regarded each other warily, an accord was struck over the course of long debate.

In combining the twin gods' knowledge of Hysh with Malerion's knowledge of Ulgu, they deduced that the two realms were inextricably linked – and that there was theoretically a penumbral sub-realm between the two. It was a leap of meta-logic that led them to Uhl-Gysh, the Hidden Gloaming, where they found common ground. This was the first step in a massively ambitious plan that would end in a loose alliance – and, more importantly, the eventual entrapment of the Chaos God who had doomed their race.

The imprisonment of Slaanesh was the crowning glory of the alliance between the aelven gods. It was a work of such impossible scale and ambition that, for the aelves, it defined the Age of Myth. As well as ensnaring their nemesis, it allowed both the twin gods and their Ulgu-dwelling counterparts to rescue souls, one by one, from within the god that had consumed them.

The first of those aelven souls to be siphoned from Slaanesh's essence became known as the Idoneth, which means 'extreme seclusion' in the aelven tongue. They were so badly scarred by their incarceration – both physically and spiritually – that they were close to madness, and the vast majority of their offspring were born with swiftly withering souls. In his grief, Teclis nearly destroyed them all, but at the last, Tyrion stayed his hand. The Idoneth fled to the deepest, darkest places they could find and there began a new life, one day to rise again. Other groups of aelven souls were saved from within Slaanesh, ranging in appearance from the monstrous to the angelic. The most stable and sane of all these races were the Lumineth.

RISE OF ENLIGHTENMENT

For a time, Hysh was idyllic. The innate benefits of the Realm of Light saturated Lumineth society at every level. They found a thousand ways to prosper, drinking deep of the knowledge to be exploited there. But in their haste to ascend, they left behind those earthly concepts that might have kept them from the disasters that followed.

Years slid by as the twin gods rescued ever more souls from within the captive entity Slaanesh. Their skill in penumbral magic, already strong enough to bind a deity, was refined to the point that they could reincarnate their lost brethren hale and whole – no longer were their attempts haunted by cursed anatomies or hollow souls. The Lumineth created a culture of betterment that founded nine Great Nations across Hysh, one in every paradise save the mind-searing landscape of Haixiah. Tyrion and Teclis thrilled at the sight, for in the Lumineth, they saw aelven times of yore reborn. Perhaps, in their eagerness to find kinship, they subconsciously averted their gaze from the seed of darkness within these numinous beings. For it is in the nature of light to cast a shadow, and where it shines brightest, darkness can fester and grow strong.

The Lumineth spread their influence across the Ten Paradises with sublime efficacy. Some sought to conquer the vistas of the mind, their bodies seated cross-legged as their spirits roamed far and wide. Others travelled the lands, making beautiful tomes of the knowledge they found in the fields of cartography, biology, botany, history and more. These pioneers and warriors did not slaughter those monsters and savage creatures they encountered, for they considered such tactics barbaric. Instead, they tamed the beasts of the land where possible, left them to their own devices if that was not viable, or, if the creatures were particularly predatory, manoeuvred them through Realmgates to other, less enlightened realms.

It was child's play for the aelves to learn new languages, sciences and forms of art. Even the meagrest talent blossomed into mastery after only a few short weeks of study. With aesthetics playing such a large part in the aelven mindset, the Lumineth's citadels, palaces and spires became taller and more ambitious with each passing year, gleaming in the bright Hyshian light. The routes between the Ten Paradises were easy to find; for one attuned to the magical nature of the realm itself, all it took was to simply think of a bridge of light, and that gleaming span would appear.

With the natural hazards of Hysh placated or at least documented, the various academic bodies of Hysh turned their gaze to those around them. They often sought to outdo one another as their bodies of work grew more complex. Many a friendly rivalry cropped up, driving both sides to ever greater feats; one school of thought might be in contravention of another and hence endeavour to outshine its opposite, whilst a practitioner of a particular art form might strive to become pre-eminent.

The teachings of the Lumineth masters, focused around the escalating pursuit of higher knowledge, was slowly formalised by the eldest of their number into the Teclamentari, or Teclian Ladder. Shown diagrammatically, each 'rung' of this ladder was a stage of mastery over the mind and soul. To graduate from one to another required the passing of a strenuous mental test; though not all survived with their sanity intact, the rewards were great indeed. Those who climbed to the higher rungs became so enlightened that they seemed almost ethereal, literally glowing with inner wisdom.

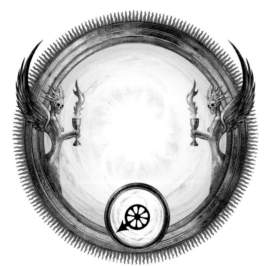

PRISMATICALLY PURE

The purest concentration of magic in Hysh travels the realm as beams of yellow-white illumination. These rays move so quickly that, initially, their power could not be trapped or siphoned. Only after Teclis taught the seers of Hysh the secret to harnessing the rare beams was the energy they contained finally mastered. When caught, the light transforms into magically translucent prisms, a realmstone called Hysh crystal or aetherquartz. Once solidified, the realmstone forms mysterious symmetrical patterns and rune-like symbols, although only the aelves of Hysh have thus far made any sense of the esoteric configurations. The quartz-like realmstone has strange prismatic powers that can be used to concentrate or dissipate magical energy. During the Age of Sigmar, Teclis constructed the enormous Tower of Prios out of aetherquartz, using its purifying beam to lessen the effects of Nagash's necroquake in Hysh.

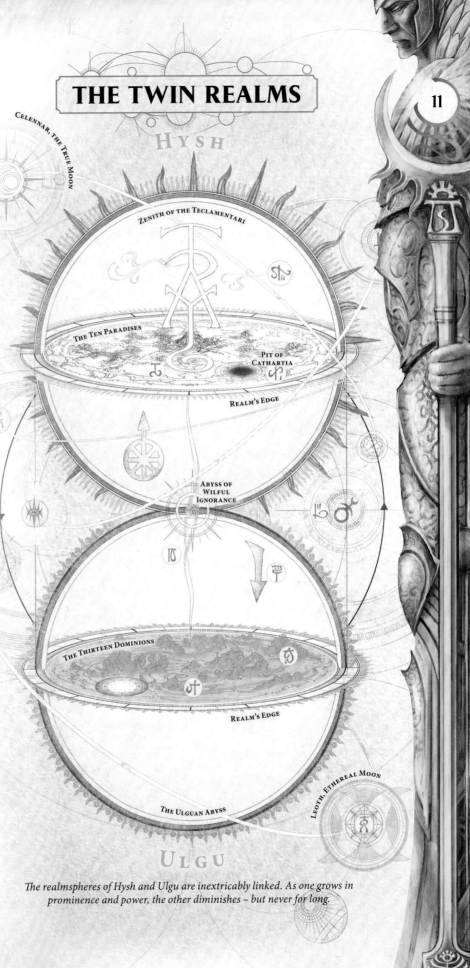

THE TWIN REALMS

It was said that to reach the zenith of the Teclian Ladder was to ascend to a higher plane altogether, though not even Teclis had accomplished that feat. So integral was this system to Lumineth society that one high up in the ways of the Teclamentari could order one less advanced to do as he bade, even should the former be a hermit and the latter a king.

Then came the revelation of Hyshian realmstone. The magic of Hysh did not naturally coalesce into deposits; instead, it appeared as beams of energy that were all but impossible to predict or catch as they shot across the firmament. It was Archmage Teclis who first magically transmuted this energy into a solid state. When cut and prepared correctly, this 'aetherquartz' remained a stable form of Hyshian light, the energies of the realm endlessly reflecting and refracting within its crystalline mass without dissipating.

Those who came into contact with glowing aetherquartz crystal would absorb its power and illumination to become enlightened in mind, body and spirit. This is the only way that the aetherquartz would ever grow dim – by having its potential siphoned off by a living soul. Over time, however, its inner light would be replaced by the emotions it would drain from its host, for such is the symmetry and balance of Hysh: when one energy diminishes, it must be replaced by another.

It was not long before the harnessing of aetherquartz became a focus of aelven artifice. Jewellery was made to display it, sword hilts were made to house it and small crystals were even worn as piercings or held under the tongue so as to better transfer its gifts directly to the owner. It raised the intellect of those who wore it to new heights, lent dexterity and focus to those warriors who sought its aid and gave a critical boost to aspirants hoping to ascend the Teclian Ladder to pass their trials. Spent aetherquartz, redolent with raw emotion, was disposed of in the chasm-city known as Cathartia. All seemed well, but with unbound power comes the insidious taint of temptation.

The realmspheres of Hysh and Ulgu are inextricably linked. As one grows in prominence and power, the other diminishes – but never for long.

THE TOPPLING OF THE SPIRES

The Spirefall – or the Ocari Dara, as the aelves call it – was perhaps the inevitable consequence of the Lumineth scaling such dizzying heights of ambition. Starting with cruel whispers, it escalated to a cataclysmic war of magic that saw the servants of Slaanesh breach reality and the Age of Chaos swiftly take hold amongst the Great Nations.

Supercharged by aetherquartz, the unbridled progress and success of the Lumineth had an intoxicating effect on the aelven psyche. Competition grew ever fiercer, and the struggle to corner the market for the raw stuff of aetherquartz became intense. Intrigue and game-playing turned to skulduggery and sabotage, but, as yet, none dared openly admit to their weakness.

Always the Lumineth climbed higher, seeking to escape the earthly demands of the body and the lands themselves. Many began to forsake sleep, seeing the business of rest as a waste of valuable time that could be better spent in the furtherance of craft or, at the very least, in mind-expanding meditation. To spend a third of each day with eyes closed – perhaps even snoring like a base human or duardin – was considered a boorish habit that the truly enlightened could do without. Yet by rising ever higher, they courted a hidden existential danger. The ultimate truth of the Teclian Ladder was that to reach its top was to travel to the highest point of Hysh, which was just as much the edge of the realmsphere as the Perimeter Inimical – and just as lethal.

Over time, an insidious fever of pride took hold, with some aelven masters openly attempting to outdo their rivals in all things. Others were subtler, casting sly aspersions at those who blatantly showed their excellence. Though none were so gauche as to point it out directly, they went to great lengths to ensure their towers were slightly taller and more grandiose, their robes whiter, their spells cleaner and more precise in effect than those of their fellows. Masters of the Teclamentari who held forth about their knowledge and experience would obsess over

how many listened to their lectures in comparison to those of their contemporaries. Artisans made progressively more impressive and powerful magical masterpieces, especially in the nation of Syar, where the creation of incredible works of art had become a speciality. Mages, seers and theurgists of all kinds devised works of arcane genius, some of which were spells so destructive they could unravel the fabric of reality. They swore to one another that they would never use these ultimate weapons, that they were there simply as deterrents in case the spectre of Chaos ever fell upon their civilisation. But under the civility and manners of every debate, there were implications and subtexts that were as sharp as blades, for the aelves craft even conversation with flair, intellect and, sometimes, spite.

In the folded psyches of those most besotted with the quest for aetherquartz, the sibilant hisses of the Dark Prince turned into whispers, then words, then haunting suggestions that played upon the edges of the subconscious. These souls looked darkly at their closest rivals, ever vigilant for weaknesses and secretly exploring ways to bring them low. When a lauded composer of lumin-symphonies vilified his rival, saying his contemporary's muse was daemonic in origin, it began a cycle of accusation and flared tempers. Sides were taken, vows of vengeance were sworn and the affair blossomed into outright violence that saw the towers of the two rivals toppled. Alas, Tyrion and Teclis were abroad at this time, tending to the arcane wards of the Hidden Gloaming and treating with the Pantheon of Order. They had long believed their kin were far

above acts of self-destruction. They could not have been more wrong.

Word soon spread that the taboo of inter-school conflict had been broken. Rumours of daemonology circulated high and low, for the notion was not only horrifying enough to be titillating for the gossips of high society, it was also a useful tool for blackening rivals' names. Though the accusations turned out to be baseless, the fear and repulsion conjured by the very mention of daemonic influence sent ripples of paranoia through every stratum of Lumineth society. Premises were searched, privileges revoked and advantage taken on the flimsiest pretext. It was the spark that set alight the kindling, inflaming rivalries that had grown ever fiercer over the course of the Age of Myth.

In the space of a few short weeks, slander turned to outright attack in every aelven province. This was nothing so coarse as physical violence; rather, spells were woven first to denigrate, then to harm. Cantrips worked in secret became hexes cast in the open; rites and rituals were designed not only to wound but to banish – and, ultimately, to kill. A dizzying escalation took hold, a surging tide of repressed emotion bursting out like pus from a lanced boil. Before they knew it, the Lumineth were calling up the direst enchantments and most powerful magical weapons at their disposal – even those they swore they would never use – and unleashing them upon their hated rivals.

The magical cataclysm that followed became known as the Spirefall, for it was not just the Lumineth that paid the price of their tempestuous outbursts but the lands they called home. With their abilities bolstered to supernatural levels by the wholesale consumption of aetherquartz, the aelves used spells so destructive that they blasted apart palaces with a single phrase and worked arcane miracles so powerful that they flattened entire districts. The most potent spells obliterated cities, filled the skies with ash and choked rivers with the bodies of the dead, their afterquakes shaking apart even the mountains on the horizon. In places, reality itself was ripped apart, the veil between the material world and the Realm of Chaos torn wide open.

Pouring through came the daemons of Slaanesh. They had waited long for the moment when aelven pride would give them a crack to exploit and lever open so wide that the daemons born of their excess could be held back no longer. Great was their glee upon seeing the once-proud glory of Hysh laid low in so spectacular a fashion. They frolicked and danced amongst the carnage, preying on those aelves still reeling from the doom they had inflicted upon themselves.

In those few places where level heads prevailed, the Lumineth fought back, islands of sanity in a maelstrom of disaster. Were it not for Tyrion's martial genius, perhaps all would have been lost. Even so, the vast majority of Hysh was so thoroughly consumed by civil war – and the daemonic invasion that it had allowed to manifest – that the land shattered and cracked, devastated by the fires of battle and rampant magical energies that wracked the landscape. The realm itself cried out, for its elegant paradises had been turned into war-torn hellscapes.

So began the Age of Chaos in Hysh, the vengeance of Slaanesh writ large. For centuries, the realm suffered like never before.

THE ELEMENTAL PACT

Lumineth society was ravaged by the insanity of the Spirefall. Its salvation came not from the realm but from the wisdom of the aether outside it. Undertaking a great void-quest, Archmage Teclis found a way to commune with the geomantic spirits of the realms. It was the beginning of a new order for the mages and warriors of Hysh.

Whilst Hysh's citadels toppled into the dust, Tyrion led the realm's defence against a hundred Chaos incursions and more. Archmage Teclis was nowhere to be found. At first, this was seen by the Lumineth as abandonment, for his sagacity was sorely needed in those times of strife and wanton displays of power. His people cried out to him, begging him to change the course of fate and keep them from utter destruction.

Teclis felt every word resonate within his spirit, though he did not reply. Though his body sat meditating in the wilderness of Haixiah, his mind travelled far, even into the aetheric void. Out there in the darkness, he spoke mind-to-mind with beings not of the realmspheres and found new wisdom. In his aetheric communion with the spirit of Hysh's true moon, Celennar, Teclis made an incredible breakthrough. It allowed a critical shift in perspective from that of a centralised body of thought to an existence that orbited another – a spirit known as an aelementor.

Were it not for the fact that Teclis had been born a twin, he might never have managed to find common ground with so unearthly a spirit as that moon-essence. Yet Celennar recognised something of a kindred spirit in Teclis, for he had a duality in his soul, just as the moon shared a duality with the sun-realm it orbited. Though part of Celennar's odd sentience was content to sing with the music of the spheres, they kept a sliver of themselves alert as Teclis spoke of the dilemma facing his race.

A full month later, when Teclis returned to the remnants of his people, at his side came Celennar, glowing brightly with the reflected magic of the Hyshian realmsphere. Together, the two gathered the most selfless and repentant of their people – those who truly sought a way out of the obsession that had so nearly doomed their race. These were

to be the first of the Hyshian aelves to learn the art of bonding with the realm itself.

The founders of the aelementiri temples were chosen by Teclis for a number of factors – first of all, their humility. These were mages who had tasted the dizzying power of the Teclamentari's upper reaches but had willingly put it aside, realising that there were some secrets mortal minds were not meant to know. Some amongst them had toppled from the heights of their addiction to enlightenment during the Spirefall, crashing into the bedrock of reality; yet, through sheer grit, they had survived. Many of them were scarred in body and soul by centuries of war against the daemons of Chaos, but still they fought. Over time, it was these hardened souls who were to become the first true Realm-lords.

Those who had been burned by the fires of their own hubris had gained a vital measure of perspective. Only by putting their desires to one side, by looking outside themselves for a new power, could they rise from the ashes. Teclis taught these supplicants to speak to the geomantic spirits of Hysh, just as he himself had learnt to speak with Celennar. Even as the realm itself could take no more and the Ten Paradises began to crumble away, a new hope rose to unite them.

This was the beginning of the fabled Wars of the Reinvention, the long, bloody and strife-filled period in which the Lumineth overcame daemons both within and without and, in doing so, became one with Hysh. Those seeking enlightenment had to choose an aelementor as their spiritual lode – be it a mountain spirit for a would-be Alarith or light itself for those who sought the zenith high above the clouds. Before approaching their new patron, they would divest themselves of all that they had accrued, whether material possessions, preconceptions or strictures of knowledge. Then, the aelementiri trial would begin in earnest. The supplicant had to endure the elements, even in the harshest natural cycles. One who would become one with the river might spend a year listening to its wisdom even in times of flood, swim its length out to sea and back to the source, then, at the last, submerge themselves entirely, tying weights to their limbs and forcing themselves to sink. If the river's spirit deemed them worthy, it would allow them to breathe underwater and buoy them back up to the surface. They would then take a new name, worship at its riverside temple and carry a measure of its spirit magic in their souls. Those whom the river deemed unworthy would simply drown.

In the years since the Reinvention, the aelementiri have founded hundreds of temples. There are some amongst the aelves of Ulgu who maintain that the aelementiri, in devoting themselves so wholly to their patrons, have simply swapped one obsession for another. Nevertheless, the Ten Paradises have gradually rebuilt a semblance of their former glory, tempered by humility and a yen for cooperation – outwardly, at least. Post-Reinvention, the Lumineth are rising, and those who seek to stop them face not only the arcane skill of the aelves but the wrath of mighty Hysh itself.

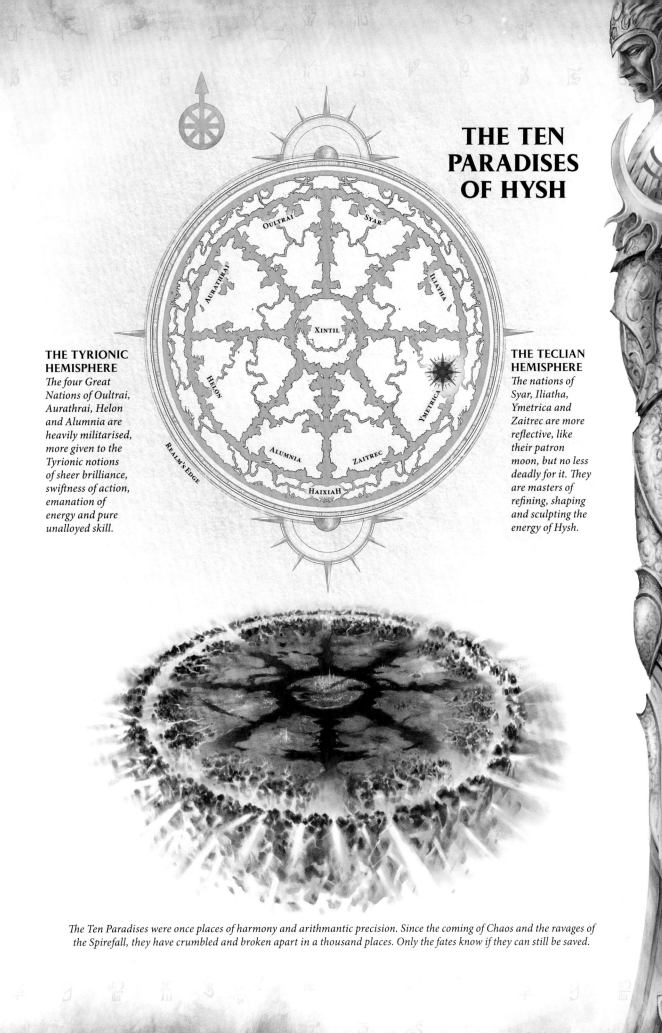

THE TEN PARADISES OF HYSH

OULTRAI

SYAR

AURATHRAI

ILIATHA

XINTIL

HELON

YMETRICA

ALUMNIA

ZAITREC

REALM'S EDGE

HAIXIAH

THE TYRIONIC HEMISPHERE

The four Great Nations of Oultrai, Aurathrai, Helon and Alumnia are heavily militarised, more given to the Tyrionic notions of sheer brilliance, swiftness of action, emanation of energy and pure unalloyed skill.

THE TECLIAN HEMISPHERE

The nations of Syar, Iliatha, Ymetrica and Zaitrec are more reflective, like their patron moon, but no less deadly for it. They are masters of refining, shaping and sculpting the energy of Hysh.

The Ten Paradises were once places of harmony and arithmantic precision. Since the coming of Chaos and the ravages of the Spirefall, they have crumbled and broken apart in a thousand places. Only the fates know if they can still be saved.

STADIUM
ILLUMINATOS

FAKIR'S
WASTE

THE BLEND

SYLL'ESSKAN
WASTES

THALUIN
RECLAMATION

THE LEAPS

GLORIANI'S
ECHO

THE LAST
PORTAL

TEMPER'S
FLARE

DOOM OF
SPIRES

XINTIL

EXTRAPOLATED
SPUR

VAROUR'S
LESSON

COAST OF LUCID DREAMS

THE GIRDLESEA

ILIATHA

HANORI
SEAL

CEYLIAN
STORMBREAK

TOR
KITISE

BREAKING
POINT

TOR QULIAN

LACOI'S
TRIUMPH

SHIMMERSEA

FRACTAL
FJORDS

COAST OF PRISMS

TOR
ILIDRETH

ARCH
OF MEN

TOR
AMUN

RUINS OF
AILLIANIS

CLASH OF
NATIONS

LAKE
PERPENDICULAR

TOR
ELID

REVELATIA

REVELATION DESERT

ALABASTER
CANALS

AROTH
STRONGPOINT

GLIMMERING INLETS

QUISLAI BRACE

MOUNT
AVALENOR

CRAKENMAW
CHASM

HEDONIST'S
REVEL

MALANIA'S
LAMENT

CYTHON'S
BITE

BLACKPIT
REALMGATE

TOURMALINE
SPIRES

HEL
CLASH

THE PILLAR
OF TRUTH

ELDOIR RANGE

AVALENORIA

SCINTILLA FALLS

SETTLER'S GAIN

THE CRUMBLING COAST

THE GREAT
VINDICATION

YMETRICA COREWARD

VERTIGINOUS PEAKS

THE GIRDLESEA

GLIB
STRETCH

LOTHIL DELT

ELTHONDU

THE
PIERCING
LAKES

TOR
XILLION

SELENI COAST

SARATRAI
CHASM

ILARU JETTIES

SUNDRAKE
CREST

IL'DOSTILYA'S
FOLLY

RUINLIGHT SOUND

GREAT DAIXO RIVER

FALLEN
CYRIA

TYRION'S
FLAW

DRAKSPINE PEAKS

CYRIAN
WASTES

MELUVANE

SHATTERING CLIFFS

STOICAL
VAST

TOR XILLION

One of the many broken cities gracing
the coasts, Tor Xillion fights bravely
but is still besieged by Chaos invaders.

CRYSTAL
CAVERNS

THE
NOTHINGS

CELENNAR'S
GIFT

SEAPORT
MATAH

MOILA
VARDAN

UAIMH
WHIRLWAY

LUNEGLOW

ZAITREC

ISTRIN
ARCGATE

MER ZAIMETRICA

CARAVANSERAI TRADE ROUTE

MONCHILDRANI

THE
BEAK

YMETRICAN GEOSEGMENT

CORRUPTED
CRATERS

ZOROSTRAMARAN
DESERT

THE
BROKEN
DELUGE

THE
BITE

TRANQUIL
PLAIN

LECA
BEACH

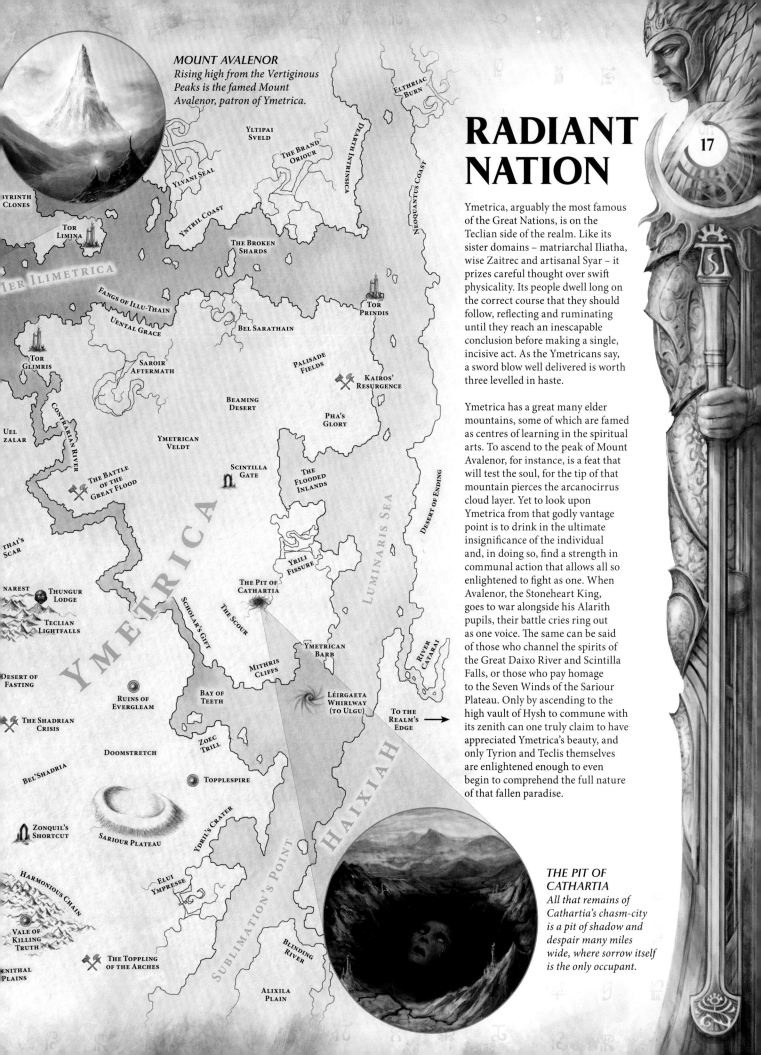

MOUNT AVALENOR
Rising high from the Vertiginous Peaks is the famed Mount Avalenor, patron of Ymetrica.

RADIANT NATION

Ymetrica, arguably the most famous of the Great Nations, is on the Teclian side of the realm. Like its sister domains – matriarchal Iliatha, wise Zaitrec and artisanal Syar – it prizes careful thought over swift physicality. Its people dwell long on the correct course that they should follow, reflecting and ruminating until they reach an inescapable conclusion before making a single, incisive act. As the Ymetricans say, a sword blow well delivered is worth three levelled in haste.

Ymetrica has a great many elder mountains, some of which are famed as centres of learning in the spiritual arts. To ascend to the peak of Mount Avalenor, for instance, is a feat that will test the soul, for the tip of that mountain pierces the arcanocirrus cloud layer. Yet to look upon Ymetrica from that godly vantage point is to drink in the ultimate insignificance of the individual and, in doing so, find a strength in communal action that allows all so enlightened to fight as one. When Avalenor, the Stoneheart King, goes to war alongside his Alarith pupils, their battle cries ring out as one voice. The same can be said of those who channel the spirits of the Great Daixo River and Scintilla Falls, or those who pay homage to the Seven Winds of the Sariour Plateau. Only by ascending to the high vault of Hysh to commune with its zenith can one truly claim to have appreciated Ymetrica's beauty, and only Tyrion and Teclis themselves are enlightened enough to even begin to comprehend the full nature of that fallen paradise.

THE PIT OF CATHARTIA
All that remains of Cathartia's chasm-city is a pit of shadow and despair many miles wide, where sorrow itself is the only occupant.

Map labels:

BYRINTH CLONES

TOR LIMINA

IER ILIMETRICA

FANGS OF ILLU-THAIN

UENTAL GRACE

TOR GLIMRIS

UEL ZALAR

SAROIR AFTERMATH

CONTRARIAN RIVER

THE BATTLE OF THE GREAT FLOOD

THAI'S SCAR

NAREST

THUNGUR LODGE

TECLIAN LIGHTFALLS

DESERT OF FASTING

RUINS OF EVERGLEAM

THE SHADRIAN CRISIS

BEL'SHADRIA

DOOMSTRETCH

ZONQUIL'S SHORTCUT

SARIOUR PLATEAU

HARMONIOUS CHAIN

VALE OF KILLING TRUTH

ENITHAL PLAINS

THE TOPPLING OF THE ARCHES

ELUI YMPRESSE

YDRIL'S CRATER

TOPPLESPIRE

ZOEC TRILL

BAY OF TEETH

SCHOLAR'S GIFT

THE SCOUR

MITHRIS CLIFFS

THE PIT OF CATHARTIA

YMETRICAN BARB

LÉIRGAETA WHIRLWAY (TO ULGU)

TO THE REALM'S EDGE →

SUBLIMATION'S POINT

BLINDING RIVER

ALIXILA PLAIN

HAIXIAH

YMETRICA

YMETRICAN VELDT

SCINTILLA GATE

BEAMING DESERT

THE FLOODED INLANDS

YRILI FISSURE

PHA'S GLORY

PALISADE FIELDS

KAIROS' RESURGENCE

BEL SARATHAIN

THE BROKEN SHARDS

YNTRIL COAST

YLVANI SEAL

YLTIPAI SVELD

THE BRAND ORIOUR

DEARTH INTRINSICA

ELTHRIAC BURN

NEOQUANTUS COAST

TOR PRINDIS

LUMINARIS SEA

DESERT OF ENDING

RIVER CATARAJ

A WAR OF THE SPIRIT

Though the scions of Hysh were almost entirely absent from the Realmgate Wars, having their own affairs to look to after the disasters of the Ocari Dara, the ripples of death magic that cascaded across the Mortal Realms spurred them into action. Without them to cast their blessed light, darkness would surely triumph.

Even as he taught the Lumineth how to commune with the spirits of the realm, Teclis cast his far-seeing eyes across the Ten Paradises. So vast were these lands that this feat threatened to overwhelm his godly mind. But by identifying those areas of Hysh he considered to be salvageable from the Chaos incursions, he was able to coordinate an ordered retreat from those that were irredeemable and slowly shape that withdrawal into a grand defence. Working with his growing aelementiri temples to ensure that Tyrion's new military orders could call upon support from the realm itself, Teclis and his twin rebuilt a cogent war effort.

With the genius of the gods behind them, the aelves fought to sanctify the areas that had been brought so close to utter destruction. Sealing off those parts of the Great Nations where reality had split, they burned vast geomantic symbols into the lands to ensure they were rendered stable. The strictures of war and magic that they laid down – amongst them the Decree Tyrionic that founded the Vanari – have shaped the Lumineth warhosts ever since.

THE ARCANUM OPTIMAR

The Reinvention had altered Lumineth society entire, their new-found sense of unity giving them hope. But the battle against the invading hordes of Chaos was far from over. Worse still, the forces of Death were on the rise; just as the Hyshian nations were recovering from the daemonic invasion, macabre omens began to manifest across the lands.

A realm of symbolism ever since its first coalescence, Hysh manifested the signs of the Time of Tribulations as a sickening body sprouts the symptoms of disease. The skies shifted to portray burning skulls, the skeletons of snakes slithered

with new life to chew their own tails, scatterings of bone fell from the skies and crimson mists billowed across the deserts to paint fallen alabaster statues red like flayed corpses. The Zaitreci spoke of the ghost of an ancient moon haunting the cosmos, preying on the secrets of the weak, and of strange vibrations in the motes of amethyst magic that they observed in the course of their investigations. It was clear to all who studied them that the omens and portents were emanating from Shyish, the Realm of Death.

In their scrying, the Lumineth ascertained that the forces of Sigmar, as well as the teeming warbands of the Dark Gods and the idiot savants of Destruction, were moving against Nagashizzar. The aelves did not commit any real military strength to the turmoil in Shyish, for they were still consumed by the painfully slow reclamation of Hysh. Instead, by the order of Teclis, they raised structures of aetherquartz that would lessen any necromantic emanations that assailed their lands. It was a paltry defence against that which was to come, but the Lumineth, still rebuilding after the disastrous events of the Spirefall centuries earlier, had little other choice.

No sooner had the Hyshian aelves re-established a semblance of control in the heartlands of their realm than the Shyish necroquake broke

across the cosmos. Deathly magic cascaded across Hysh, as it did all of the Mortal Realms. In every one of the Ten Paradises, the dead roamed hungry and evil of aspect. The unwise, the proud and the incautious soon joined them, falling to the claws of Nighthaunt processions or Deadwalker hordes – though the Lumineth were swift of foot and quick of thought, the dead never tired, and their numbers were legion.

The vast majority of the Lumineth survived only through unity. They had been warned of such an encroachment, and by using the tall pillars and obelisks of aetherquartz that Teclis had had them raise in preparation, they held the worst of the deathly disaster at bay. Yet the magical backlash meant that many of the spells cast by the Lumineth became sentient; intended to destroy the threats to the fragile peace they had forged, these spells started to roam the lands. The Arcanum Optimar had begun.

The wastes of Hysh were now prowled by predatory magical entities that, though they owed no direct allegiance to the Dark Gods, were just as lethal as their chaotic equivalents. The effect this magical disorder had on the Lumineth psyche was profound. It was obvious now that the other realms could not be trusted to look to their own affairs, and with tyrants such as Nagash able to mastermind reality-shaking rites of such a magnitude that they even assailed Hysh, the aelves no longer had the luxury of their previous isolationism.

THE ETERNAL THREAT

Amidst it all, the prospect of Slaanesh's eventual escape loomed large. Both Tyrion and Teclis had been shaken by the effects of the necroquake upon Hysh, but though the curse of undeath that had spilled across the Ten Paradises had been horrific, there was one fate that they considered darker still. It was possible that the cosmic disruption caused by Shyish's inversion had disturbed the precise metamagical formulae with which they had bound their nemesis, the Dark Prince, in the prison of Uhl-Gysh.

The twin gods gathered in council with Malerion and his long-time advisor, Morathi, upon the strange islands of matter that hovered in the Hidden Gloaming. Malerion revealed that he had been scrutinising their paradoxical prison of light and shadow ever since the first ripple of the necroquake, and still it held true. Tyrion had no cause to believe his own works were flawed and nodded in agreement – he had reached the same conclusion. Morathi, by contrast, was not convinced. She spoke passionately about the fact that a new disaster was inevitable, saying they could no more hold a god of Chaos indefinitely than they could stop the passage of time itself. The gods of light and shadow departed at an impasse, though Morathi's speech had left its mark on one of their number.

Upon returning to Hysh, Teclis spoke at length with Celennar about the matter. He believed the High Oracle of Khaine had a cogent point. Chaos was immortal, as were the sins and flaws of men, duardin and aelves. One fell day, Slaanesh would rise again. The more he dwelt on the matter, the more it seemed inevitable. So it was that Teclis gathered his allies and marshalled the armies of Ymetrica into a great vanguard, with those of Syar, Iliatha and Zaitrec not far behind.

The Lumineth would go out into the Mortal Realms and seal those sites where reality thinned, shoring up its defences as they had in Hysh. They would make it so that the daemons of Slaanesh and his brothers in darkness could no more break through their wards than a shoal of ripjaws could swim through a metres-thick dam of obstinite. It was a noble endeavour, but it would prove to have a great many complications of its own.

The Tourmaline Spires were the site of a critical alliance between the forces of Hysh and Azyr that would bear fruit on scores of different war fronts.

THE LUMINETH HOSTS

The Vanari are the foremost military body of the Lumineth, and they form the bright core of their warhosts. Consisting of tightly bonded phalanxes of Auralan infantry – most prominent among them the pike-wielding Wardens and keen-eyed Sentinel archers – they are supported by the glorious cavalry of the Vanari Dawnriders. These shining companies glow with light as they take to the field, bringing hope to their allies and panic to their foes.

Each Vanari warhost is composed of several smaller battalions. These are formed around the Decree Tyrionic, principles of efficiency and martial optimisation laid down by the Lord of Lumination himself. It is common to see as many Sentinel archers as spear-wielding Wardens, the one stationed behind the other to ensure the enemy is imperilled at range and outclassed at close quarters. Those enemies who attack in strength are assailed by the lightning assaults of the Dawnriders, cavaliers who specialise in fighting when outnumbered, allowing them to balance the odds for when the foe reaches the main Vanari battle line. The main body of the host is further reinforced by the aelementiri temples, who fight on their own terms but invariably work in concert with the wider Lumineth army.

The first such warhost seen abroad in the Mortal Realms was the Teclian Vanguard, led by not only the master archmage Teclis but also the Light of Eltharion.

THE TECLIAN VANGUARD OF YMETRICA

The Teclian Vanguard comprises no fewer than three Auralan Legions, reinforced by two Dawnrider Lances and a temple of Alarith led by Avalenor, the Stoneheart King.

The Vanguard was the first major Lumineth force to have ventured through Hysh's portals to join the wider wars of the Mortal Realms. Whilst many of their fellow Great Nations were still debating the best course of action to oppose the forces of Chaos as the necroquake raged, this small but lethal warhost was already in the thick of battle, fighting and dying in those conflicts Teclis judged most critical of all.

THE LIGHT OF ELTHARION

AURALAN LEGION	AURALAN LEGION
HOST OF LOTHIL DELT	*TAZALARI BLADES*
Scinari Cathallar	Scinari Cathallar
Yr'inae of the Sheared Soul	*Lhariselle of Aendloc*
Auralan Wardens	Auralan Wardens
Saratrai Longspears	*Ilaru's Protectors*
Auralan Wardens	Auralan Wardens
Guardians of Aillia	*Stalwarts of Tor Ilidreth*
Auralan Wardens	Auralan Wardens
Bladeweavers of Cerai Thenn	*Conscience of Bel'Shadria*
Auralan Sentinels	Auralan Sentinels
Matah's First Archers	*Zonquil's Justice*
Auralan Sentinels	Auralan Sentinels
Brethren Immaculate	*Sharpeyes of Elui Ympresse*
Auralan Sentinels	Auralan Sentinels
Eyes of Tor Amun	*Zoec Trill Sunguard*

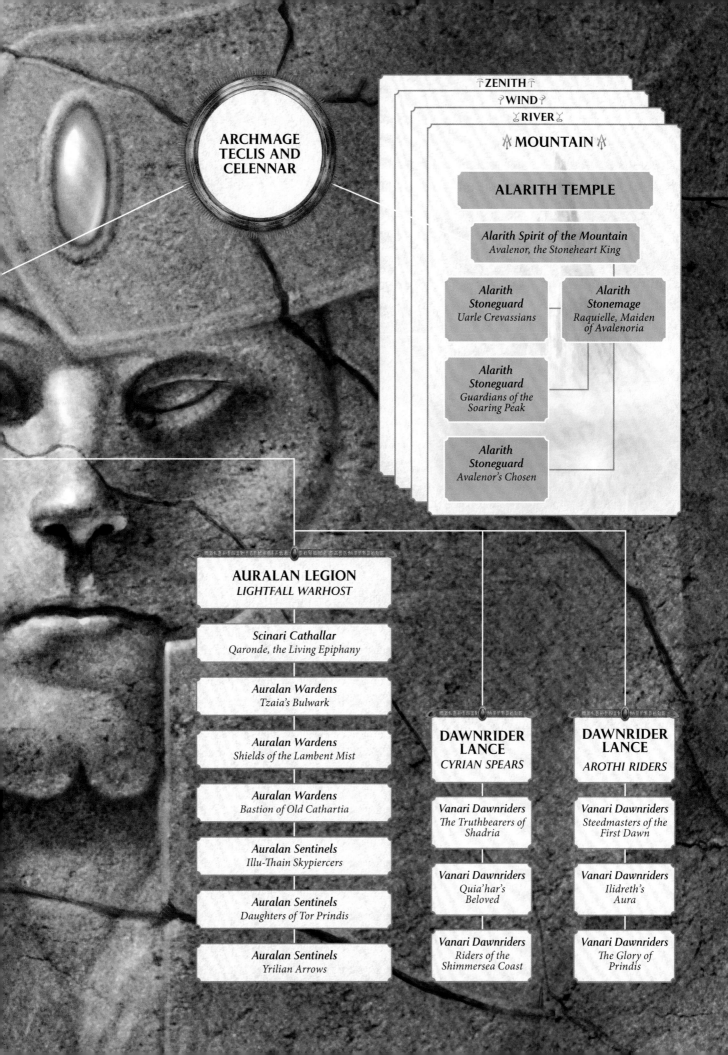

ARCHMAGE TECLIS AND CELENNAR

☥ ZENITH ☥
⚶ WIND ⚶
⚯ RIVER ⚯
⚶ MOUNTAIN ⚶

ALARITH TEMPLE

Alarith Spirit of the Mountain
Avalenor, the Stoneheart King

Alarith Stoneguard
Uarle Crevassians

Alarith Stonemage
Raquielle, Maiden of Avalenoria

Alarith Stoneguard
Guardians of the Soaring Peak

Alarith Stoneguard
Avalenor's Chosen

AURALAN LEGION
LIGHTFALL WARHOST

Scinari Cathallar
Qaronde, the Living Epiphany

Auralan Wardens
Tzaia's Bulwark

Auralan Wardens
Shields of the Lambent Mist

Auralan Wardens
Bastion of Old Cathartia

Auralan Sentinels
Illu-Thain Skypiercers

Auralan Sentinels
Daughters of Tor Prindis

Auralan Sentinels
Yrilian Arrows

DAWNRIDER LANCE
CYRIAN SPEARS

Vanari Dawnriders
The Truthbearers of Shadria

Vanari Dawnriders
Quia'har's Beloved

Vanari Dawnriders
Riders of the Shimmersea Coast

DAWNRIDER LANCE
AROTHI RIDERS

Vanari Dawnriders
Steedmasters of the First Dawn

Vanari Dawnriders
Ilidreth's Aura

Vanari Dawnriders
The Glory of Prindis

THE SYMMETRY OF WAR

The Lumineth muster their armies for war with the precision of a master artist arranging the interlocking parts of a mosaic. The runic mandala, as laid down by Teclis, is a touchstone for all aspects of Lumineth existence from its warriors to its craftsmen – and especially for the aelementiri, who resonate with the stuff of Hysh itself.

Since the Reinvention, the Lumineth have modulated their society around certain schools of thought that they consider to be spiritually in tune with the nature of Hysh itself. The same is true of their warhosts. Even when driven by the merciless pragmatism of battle, the Lumineth lean towards aesthetically pleasing arrangements of troops – when seen from on high, they form curves, lines and blocks that seem to spell out meaning as they flow in sympathy with the landscape. There is always logic behind these formations: their disciplines and areas of influence overlap so that no enemy force can pass through the net without facing the deadly arts of the Lumineth military. Yet there are also deeper meanings behind each warhost's composition, tied inextricably to the twin leaders of their civilisation and the complementary energies and disciplines they embody. These are represented by the Hysha-Mhensa, a runic mandala that is key to the Lumineth school of thought.

The Lumineth's core mandala has two distinct sides that echo the hemispheres of Hysh. The left-hand – or 'Tyrionic' – side of the mandala is typified by the emanation of brilliance. It is one with the sun – or, in the case of Hysh, the blindingly magical edge of the realm that forms its Perimeter Inimical. It represents inspiration, purity and quickness of action, uncomplicated by reflection and unfiltered by doubt. As such, it is synonymous with the warriors of this race, those who strike swiftly and surely without the burden of uncertainty to divert their blades. It is a grouping whose most accomplished members lead by example, even on the field of battle. Their elders include the lord and lady regents of the military, their champions, marshals and masters-at-arms. Their warriors are unusually laconic for Hyshians; communicating only in the terse and precise military cant of the

Hyshian standing armies, they are content to let their excellence speak for itself. Amongst their ranks are phalanxes of archers, spearmen, charioteers, knights, artillery specialists and scouts who fight in expert synchrony, their interlocking patterns quite beautiful to those schooled in the arts of strategy and tactical manoeuvre.

The right-hand – or 'Teclian' – side is typified by reflection, refinement and deliberation. Because of this, it is thought to be the province of the Hyshian true moon, Celennar, which reflects the light of the Realm's Edge to act as a beacon of illumination even when Ulgu's obscuring influence rides high. This hemisphere is the province of deep thinkers, and its elders include philosophers, sorcerers, mages, bards, diviners, heralds and scribes. Those of a more practical bent take the lessons of these Teclian thinkers and adapt them to the business of creation. Metalsmiths, woodshapers, healers, artisans, architects and purifiers all drink from the same font of considered knowledge as the magi who have ventured higher up the Teclamentari. These are the souls who channel and shape the clear, beaming light of Hysh to new heights of artifice, much as a prism channels a ray of pure white energy into a spectrum of dazzling colours.

There are those souls who exist between the two sides of the mandala, who are as much Teclian as they are Tyrionic. They are found in the light of the sun and

the moon at the same time, drawing strength from both to live a liminal existence. Foremost amongst these are the loreseekers, who fight as much with blades as they do with spells, often merging the two in a devastating combination. Some ancient bodies of Hyshian thought claim this synthesis of sun and moon to be the purest state of all. Nevertheless, since the coming of Tyrion and Teclis to the realm, the twin sides of the mandala have become firmly entrenched in the Lumineth psyche.

The core of the Hysha-Mhensa is a stylised combination of the four principal aspects of Hysh's nature. These are the geomantic forces with which the Lumineth aelves have made common cause. Much like the rungs of the Teclamentari, these aspects become progressively more difficult to master the higher the aspirant climbs. Though attuning oneself to a feature of the landscape is something that takes punitive months of supplication and higher thought to achieve, it is easier to engage with the spirits of those elements tied to the landscape than those free upon the wind; to hear the river is simple enough, but to commune with light itself is nigh impossible. There are tens of thousands of river warriors in the Great Nations, and there are at least a thousand Alarith who supplicate themselves to the mountains. These kindred are both numerous in comparison to those who have found an accord with the Hyshian winds. Rarest of all are those who reach the zenith, that area high above the arcanostratum cloud layer where pure light fills the upper vault of Hysh. Having transcended mortal concerns, these aelves are as much beings of thought as they are flesh and blood. Like the war-form incarnations of the aelementors themselves, they enjoy a legendary status within the ranks of the Lumineth.

RUNES OF THE LUMINETH

ZENITH

WIND

MOUNTAIN

RIVER

Thalari, the rune of Zenith, represents the world above the clouds, where light rules alone.

Oreali, the rune of Wind, represents the ephemeral force that can strike with a hurricane's anger.

Alaithi, the rune of Mountain, represents the strength of aeons and immovable resolve.

Ydriliqi, the rune of River, represents the quick-thinking, unstoppable flow of the dexterous.

Yngra, the rune of Rescue and Imprisonment, can often hint at Slaanesh's fate in Uhl-Gysh.

Senlui, the rune of Swiftness and Accuracy, is synonymous with the Vanari warhosts of Hysh.

Senthoi, the rune of Unity and Loyalty, can also mean Broken Promise, depending on context.

Ylvan, the rune of Pride, Honour and Imperfection, represents the Age of Myth.

THE RUNIC MANDALA
Though the Lumineth have many hundreds of runes, since the Reinvention, the Hysha-Mhensa has become favoured above all. It represents the union of the four principal elements of Hysh and the strength one can take from combining them all for the same cause.

A warrior or mage will typically call but one of these his patron. Only Tyrion and Teclis have souls strong enough to bond with spirits from each of the elements – Tyrion through the arts of war and Teclis through the artifice of magic.

YMETRICA – THE SCIONS OF THE PEAKS

Ymetrica is a land of lofty peaks and even loftier philosophies. The Ymetricans combine their ambition to climb ever higher with the warrior skills practised by the disciples of its many mountains. It is said that the Ymetrican armies are a gleaming white cliff against which the forces of darkness will dash themselves to pieces.

Of all those in Hysh, the people of Ymetrica are the most invested in the concept that the higher a person climbs, the easier it is for them to become enlightened. This assumption has its roots in the fact that Ymetrica has so many mountain ranges, with some of those peaks piercing the thin clouds of that realm to touch the zenithal vault high above. After Teclis brought to them the secrets of the Reinvention, the people of this land were the first to master the techniques of communing with the mountain – indeed, of communing with any geomantic spirit other than Celennar. Many of

them had walked the high passes and levitated amongst the peaks during the Age of Myth, and though they did not realise it as such, they had already begun to form something of a bond with Ymetrica's geological giants. Perhaps unsurprisingly, there are far more temples dedicated to Hysh's mountainous regions here than in any other Great Nation.

It is Ymetrica's horizon that is pierced by the great peak Avalenor, the Stoneheart King. Since the coming of the Soul Wars, their aelementiri temples have been accompanied to war not only by this most venerable of mountain spirits but by the spirits of entire chains of mountains – so much so that the phrase 'Ymetrica walks' has a literal truth to it and has become a shorthand for inevitable victory.

Owing to the inherent symmetry of Hysh, the land has as many deep chasms as it does high peaks. The Ymetricans have long believed that to descend into one of these chasms is to go on a journey of introspection and mental delving that can bring to the surface the deepest and most disturbing emotional experiences of all. To venture into such darkness is to know fear and all-consuming angst, but they appreciate that there is knowledge to be found beneath the earth and that the shadows of the subterranean realm link to a new kind of truth far below. Only those who have formed a close bond with the peaks of Ymetrica dare descend into its depths, for they know that the silver thread of wisdom that connects them to their mountainous patrons will always be there to bring them back.

The people of Ymetrica often wear triangle motifs that echo the shape of the high peak, even if they have no affiliation with a specific mountain. Some icons are capped with lateral moon crescents, others interlinked in complex patterns, but the triangle

as a visual device recurs across most Ymetrican art forms. Their people take a good deal of pride in having made an alliance with the oldest and most enduring of all Hysh's land spirits, and they will often drop into conversation the fact that they were the first to establish a long-lasting symbiosis with the realm itself.

At war, it is said that the Ymetricans think at length before acting swiftly. They tend to be the least hasty of all the Lumineth, preferring to commit only when they are sure of the land and the foe they will meet upon it. They fight with their feet firmly planted on the ground, wearing down the enemy by using their own strength against them before landing a lightning-fast coup de grâce that fells them in a single blow. In this, they seek to emulate the impervious nature of the mountain itself and the immense force of the avalanche it unleashes upon those who displease it – they repel the foe's attacks without compromising their position, crushing them without pity should the threat become too great.

Should an Ymetrican warhost commit to protecting a sacred site, perhaps to buy time for a geomantic rite or to bar access to a hidden valley, it can hold at bay a force that outnumbers its warriors a dozen times over. The trespassers will only able to set foot upon those lands once they have killed every last aelven warrior where they stand. This is no easy feat, for the Ymetricans make war with stoicism and skill, turning the very earth against the foe through their mastery of aelementiri magic. When the Spirits of the Mountain stride into the fight, acting as the hammer to the anvil of the Vanari phalanxes and their Alarith kindred, even the armoured hordes of the Chaos Gods will be broken, crushed and cast aside with grim resolve and efficiency.

SYAR – THE MAKERS OF WONDER

In the time of the Spirefall, the preternaturally talented artisans of Syar wrought utter destruction upon their homelands. Now they turn their limitless ingenuity to the business of the Mortal Realms' salvation, their famed artefacts of war set against the enemy on a score of fronts even as the Syari homelands are painstakingly rebuilt.

Syar's people have always been expert craftsmen and creators, giving form to the magical light and power so common in Hysh. To say something is of Syari quality is a high compliment indeed. The wonders of creation that the people of this land fashioned, formalised or called into being throughout the Age of Myth saw their archives and treasuries festooned with fantastical works of art. It also saw their arsenals lined with eldritch weapons and their libraries stocked with spell books that thrummed with destructive power. When the Spirefall began, those spells and weapons were wielded by the very master artisans that had sworn that they would never use them. The lands of Syar, as a result, are ravaged far more than any other Hyshian paradise.

Over the course of the Ocari Dara, the people of Syar were decimated, and the few who survived were deeply traumatised. Those Syari who lived to see the Age of Sigmar swore they would never make such destructive creations ever again, instead concentrating their efforts on the fashioning of beautiful things that were built to last. However, of late, they have strayed once more into the ways of the weaponsmith and the artisan of war. Through lengthy and reasoned debate, Teclis has convinced them that Chaos grows close to achieving complete dominion and that they have no other choice.

The aelves of Syar are usually clad in richly coloured apparel augmented with fine jewellery, yet they are never gaudy or showy in their glamour. They are typically on the forefront of Hyshian fashion, for the people of the other Great Nations know that the Syari walk the tightrope between grandeur and asceticism better than any other. Some even go so far as to decorate their flesh with the foremost teachings of Teclis in calligraphic form, using their skin as a canvas for scripted knowledge as their forebears once used illuminated manuscripts. In times of war, the Syari mete out tremendous damage from artefacts that appear as innocuous trappings of office at first glance. A jewelled daggerbrooch cuts reality itself to pierce a foe's heart, a sculpted breastplate melts the eyes of those enemies who see its gleam, while an ornamental helm sends a slicing beam of light from its crest to slash foes bodily in half. Still, these are but trinkets and magical minutiae next to the Syari weapons of the Spirefall – cataclysms given form that have long been buried in the bosom of Hysh and are only unearthed in the direst of circumstances. The people of Syar, as well as those who have faced them in battle, pray that they never need use them again.

The Syari, always on the lookout for a chance to show their supremacy in the field of craftsmanship, hold a yearly festival of artisanry in the capital city of their domain, Ar-Ennascath. Those who consider themselves expert craftsmen must brave the hellish sentient chasms and time-warping predator-spells of the Syari wastes to reach Ar-Ennascath's wondrous gates. That journey is a magical trial in its own right, and only the most gifted make it to their destination to display their exotic and beautiful creations. There are much-beloved and oft-told tales of Grungni-worshipping duardin making the journey to participate in the Syari contest, showing off the exceptional craftsmanship of their magical artefacts, only to be humbled as the Lumineth equivalents transcend conventional notions of quality altogether.

In battle, the Syari gleam brightest of all. The sheer concentration of aetherquartz they muster and fashion into their raiment of war displays their wealth for all to see. The warriors of this domain often deliberately play up their own perceived arrogance and sense of superiority to goad the enemy into an enraged attempt to take them down. Only when the potency of their magical weapons is unleashed do their adversaries realise that the Lumineth were right to think that few could triumph against many. With the superlative craftsmanship of their ancestors lending them destructive power beyond the dreams of most mortals, the foes of Syar array themselves against not only the pre-eminent craftsmen of their time but countless generations of their forebears.

ILIATHA – THE MOTHERS OF THE SPIRIT

A matriarchal society, the warriors of Iliatha put great stock in the propagation of life, both naturally and through the creation of magical simulacra. The intrigues and misdeeds that this led to in the past has forced them to have a more puritanical outlook, though they are still by far the most numerous of the Hyshian nations.

The people of Iliatha believe that it is not enough for light to simply shine; it must also regenerate and replace itself. They maintain that if illumination is finite, it can be used up, squandered or lost, much like the aetherquartz that was abused during the Age of Myth or the teaching of a soul who vanishes from history without passing on their hard-earned knowledge. They believe it is every Lumineth's duty to sire young and then bring them up in such a way that not only do they replace their parents in society, they exceed them in all things. In this way, the aelven race becomes ever more enlightened through a communal and generational change, as opposed to through individual excellence alone.

Mothers and motherhood are held sacred in Iliatha as they bring light into the world – not the light of Hysh, but the inner light of the aelven race that was once lost to Slaanesh. Those matriarchs who have not only propagated but also handed down the knowledge of the elders enjoy the highest status, as do those who shepherd the young from the womb into the radiance of Iliatha itself. They have selflessly ensured that the race is purified through their own birth rituals and the sanctity of the light born from within.

In the darkest days of Iliatha's history, the vaunting Lumineth mindset meant that many came to see childbirth as an unnecessarily painful, messy and somewhat atavistic distraction from true enlightenment. Even then, the Iliathans believed that propagation was vital, but they went about it by dividing their consciousnesses rather than generating new sentiences altogether. They perfected the arts of splitting the mind, mastering ambidexterity and focusing on two things at once. At the height of the Age of Myth, some even divided themselves bodily into doppelgängers in order to form magical clones, their magic advanced enough to create twins where only one stood before.

At one point, the practice of creating magical simulacra was commonplace, so much so that it became obsessive. Some created triple, quadruple, even quintuple versions of themselves in order to extend their own fame and influence. These beings indulged in progressively stranger and more obscure practices, safe in the knowledge that they would never betray one another's confidence.

Ultimately, their hidden experiments led to paradoxical miracles and breaches in the laws of reality. It was these that allowed Slaanesh's agents to enter, first in the form of whispering tempters, then as fully manifested hordes of daemons. So came about the Demise of Iliatha, a time that is talked about only in hushed whispers across the Great Nation. To this day, the topic of the region's fall to darkness is considered taboo even in the farthest-flung regions of Hysh.

Since the Reinvention, the creation of more than two physical iterations per soul has been outlawed throughout Iliatha and beyond. To this day, some of the original clones from the Age of Myth still exist, working in collusion with their progenitors, though in many of the severely scarred Iliathan regions, such individuals are far from welcome. In a way, however, their legacy remains in the practices and outlook of the Iliathan military.

Though bound by strict laws of genesis, Iliatha is the most populous of all the Lumineth nations. Its military forces boast a great many twins who never shared a womb but who have a potent soul-bond nonetheless. It is common practice for such clone-twins to study different military arts, to dress differently, even to take their leave of one another so as not to fall too far into the conspiracies of duplication that ravaged the Age of Myth. Yet they keep a close bond in spite of this. Many fight as Warden and Sentinel in the same Vanari warhost, so that they might protect each other's lives with bow and blade; others devote themselves to the aelementiri temples to ensure they can enjoy the companionship of their kindred spirit whilst placing another entity entirely at the heart of their existence. Having struck a balance between propagation and restraint, Iliatha has become powerful indeed.

ZAITREC – THE LAMBENT MYSTICS

The air shimmers with unreality around the Zaitreci warhosts, for this Great Nation specialises in the shaping of spells. In Zaitrec, the power of magic runs through the veins. Their sorceries come not from artefacts or formalised rites but from the essence of the Lumineth soul – even when unarmed, a Zaitreci aelf is a deadly foe.

The Lumineth of Zaitrec are exceptionally gifted in the arts of magic. Their children learn cantrips and spells at an early age; it is said that a Zaitreci aelf of ten years of age could overcome a patriarch of the Collegiate Arcane in a magical duel without suffering a single scorched hair. Perhaps there is truth to this outrageous claim, for the Zaitreci use magic with the ease that an aelf Wanderer uses a bow and arrow.

The Great Nation of Zaitrec radiates the raw energy in the earth, glowing even when Ulgu fully eclipses Hysh in power. The diffuse light of Hyshian magic shimmers in the air, as tangible as gossamer and malleable as clay to those born in those lands. The Zaitreci people will talk to the distant moons of their realm as if speaking to nearby friends, asking questions of those celestial bodies they see as functionally omniscient in all matters Hyshian. Though this has earned them a reputation for being fey and moon-touched even amongst the Teclian societies, the leaps of knowledge that the Zaitreci display have caused many to question whether the realm's moons are indeed answering them in kind.

It is through Zaitrec that Teclis wanders most frequently, for he feels more of a connection with it than any other domain. The same can be said of its people. As the adoptive sons and daughters of Teclis, the Zaitreci share his insights and mastery of the arcane. He has entrusted them with taking his teachings to the farthest corners of Hysh and beyond, venturing into the other realms as an example to less civilised peoples. It is the Zaitreci who are the most likely to be seen amongst the teeming masses of humanity, for they are ambassadors, diplomats and delegates as well as mages, and they are not above using their subtle arts to sway the course of history to their needs.

The Zaitreci are beloved of the moon spirit Celennar. Each of their mystical spire-cities claims as its patron either Celennar or one of Hysh's ethereal moons, which wax into full corporeality then fade into insubstantiality as they wane. They revere Celennar above even Teclis, and they will travel far to seek the lunasphinx's knowledge. Though they approach the duo with great ceremony, they usually pay only cursory respect to the archmage in their desire to speak to his celestial ally. Better to learn from the source than from the mouthpiece, they say. Teclis' irritation at this phrase is well hidden, but Tyrion knows of it, and it amuses him no end.

The Zaitreci consider anyone skilled in the arts of magic as worthy of respect, regardless of race or creed. They are fascinated by the various forms of magecraft practised by the other races of the cosmos, whether the formalised magic of the free cities, the innate celestial talents of the Seraphon, the runecraft of the duardin or the blood rites of their Khainite cousins. The savage faiths of the orruk, the ogor and the grot are examined from a wary distance; no doubt there is power there, but as incarnations of faith rather than skill, the Zaitreci learn of them only to better defeat them. Most feared of all is the Bad Moon worshipped by the grots of the subterranean caves, considered the natural enemy of the Zaitreci lunar cults. Though they have worked many grand rites and abjurations to ward it away, as yet that belligerent orb careens through the firmament much as it pleases.

It is common for the Zaitreci to sport lunar symbols and wear robes emblazoned with stylised images of Teclis and Celennar. Many also display the personal runes of those who have successfully communed with the celestial bodies orbiting Hysh. The most enlightened of their number sometimes have

crescent-shaped auras of light above their heads, an outward sign of their connection to the more reflective side of Hysh. Whether this is a side effect of the wisdom granted to them by their ethereal patrons or a deliberate affectation is the subject of much debate amongst the people of the other Great Nations. Still, it remains an indisputable fact that the Zaitreci are the pre-eminent spellcasters in all of Lumineth society, and though they prefer to use their arts for the betterment of their race, they are more than willing to use them to wreak havoc amongst those who would threaten them.

TO SHINE ACROSS AEONS

The history of the Realm of Light is a tragic one, for it encompasses a rise to dizzying heights, a toppling from grandeur, and then half a millennium of strife and nightmare before the light of hope could shine once more. Now, the Lumineth work with every fibre of their being to ensure the forces of Chaos cannot rule supreme.

● AGE OF MYTH ●

THE TEN PARADISES SHINE BRIGHT

Tyrion and Teclis awaken in Hysh. The Realm of Light is a place of awe-inspiring symmetry and order; in places, it is as faceted as a cut gem or as beautiful as a glass sculpture lit from within. Virginal and unsullied in its magical purity, it has many interconnecting sections that overlap and shine onto one another. For the aelven gods, to cross from one of the Ten Paradises to another is as simple as thinking a bridge of light into existence; seconds later, a shimmering plane of illumination that leads to the intended destination springs into being. The twins roam the lands in wonder, but there is still a profound sadness in their hearts, for they find no sign of their aelven kin, no matter where they look.

A PANTHEON IS BORN

Sigmar is brought to Hysh by Dracothion. The God-King weeps tears of starlight as he beholds its glory, which still glitter to this day as the Lakes of Liquid Joy. Gladly, Sigmar settles the Realm of Light with the mortal tribes he has brought under his wing. During his travels, he encounters Tyrion and Teclis, disconsolate that they can find no trace of the aelven race. He tells them all he has learnt about the Mortal Realms and informs them that a small number of aelven souls do indeed exist, albeit in Azyr. Elated to have found a familiar face and a powerful ally, Tyrion and Teclis make a formal alliance with Sigmar within a matter of days. Thus is the Pantheon of Order founded.

A GOD ENCHAINED

Tyrion and Teclis, on their explorations into the other Mortal Realms, learn that their old adversaries Malerion and Morathi have taken new form in the Realm of Shadow, for they too have escaped Slaanesh's clutches. Reasoning that

the enemy of their enemy is their friend, they make common cause in the neutral zone of Uhl-Gysh. There, a pact is made that sets in motion the most ambitious work of magic ever attempted by aelvenkind. With the aelf gods themselves as bait, Slaanesh is lured into the Hidden Gloaming then bound in chains of light and shadow. The Dark Prince is held fast, and his worshippers in the Mortal Realms cry out in despair as their prayers are met only with silence.

THE FIRST TO BE RESCUED

Teclis bends his almighty intellect to the business of rescuing the lost souls of his former people from the essence of Slaanesh. By carefully extracting their spirits into Hysh at the same time that Malerion and Morathi extract them into Ulgu, the arcane binding of light and shadow that holds Slaanesh in chains of paradox is kept in balance. Thousands of souls are retrieved, and through Teclian magic, a new aelven people is born – the Idoneth. They prove dangerously unstable, however, and flee their maker's wrath to the bottom of far-flung oceans.

A RADIANT PEOPLE

A combination of painstaking experimentation and leaps of faith sees many more types of aelf rescued, yet all prove to be flawed in some manner. When Teclis creates the first Lumineth, hope shines bright in the Ten Paradises as they settle the lands. Thriving on the illumination

of Hysh, they grow more intelligent and capable with every passing year. In the decades that follow, a glorious civilisation is born.

THE FIRST FORAYS

The beauty and potential of the Realm of Light is stunning, so much so that aelves who travel through its Realmgates find the other realms to be dull and grubby by comparison. Spending time around the primitives of the lesser realms makes the ambassadors of Hysh feel as if they are becoming tarnished – as if, day by day, they are slowly losing their birthright of enlightenment. Their intellects no longer blossom, forced as they are to simplify their thoughts and deeds so they can fit in with the denizens of the other realms. The people of Hysh take any excuse not to visit those whom they see as beneath them. With the exception of the Sigmar-worshipping human cultures that have settled in Xintil, the Hyshians tend not to stray from the Ten Paradises unless there is no other choice.

THE FIRST WARS

Dilemmas that seem impossible to the denizens of other realms are seen as laughably simple by the Hyshian ambassadors, who present the solutions as if speaking to children. When the problems of founding new nations cannot be solved with logic or arcane artifice, the Lumineth prove more than capable in the arts of war. The Hyshian soldiery outclasses that of their would-be enemies with expertly enacted feints, traps and false fronts to leave their foes stumbling and ripe for the kill.

All this unbridled excellence does not go unnoticed amongst Sigmar's burgeoning civilisations. The Lumineth earn a reputation for being arrogant and elitist. For their part, the aelves care little about the opinions of those they see as jealous yokels – as long as they could return to sup from Hysh's endless font of illumination, they are content to leave the other realms to their own meagre preoccupations.

THE CRACKS APPEAR
As with all things of beauty, the Hyshian utopia does not last forever, especially given that such wonders have a habit of attracting the ravenous attentions of the Dark Gods. With a whisper in the dreams, a suggestion borne on the wind, the captive deity Slaanesh gradually tilts the nature of Hyshian society towards a darker reflection of itself.

◉ AGE OF CHAOS ◉

THE SPIREFALL
The scourge of the Age of Chaos begins as the rivalries of the Lumineth boil over into a series of civil wars and daemon invasions that last for hundreds of years. Over the course of the Ocari Dara, works of beauty and serenity are defiled, kingly statues cast into the dirt and priceless tomes of knowledge torn to shreds or consumed by cackling, shrieking daemons of Slaanesh. The Lumineth themselves fare little better. Many of their number are tortured in horrible and inventive ways by the invading forces. Divided by their own arrogance, attacked by nightmares from a painful and murky past they thought long forgotten, the glorious cities of the Lumineth are overcome one by one.

THE PIT OF CATHARTIA
Owing to the presence of a major Realmgate leading to Ulgu at its heart, the city of Cathartia has long been considered a place of dark passions; hence, it is avoided by the Lumineth at large. The Cathallars of the Scinari are the exception. They use the Great Chasm of Cathartia as a location in which to dispose of spent aetherquartz, that dark substance that no longer shines with raw potential but harbours painful emotion in its place. Over time, the spent aetherquartz builds up, piles of dully glinting crystal mounting high in the chasm. When the Ocari Dara dawns, and a titanic battle of spells sees Cathartia cast into ruins, the chasm is overloaded with negative energy to the point that the

Realmgate is ruptured in a massive implosion. A vast hole is torn in Hysh through which shadow and emotion stream in great tides. On the other side of the portal in Ulgu, the ruined gate glows bright as it emits the brilliant light of Hysh.

SEEDS OF REDEMPTION
With the magnitude of their folly made horribly clear, the Lumineth do their best to rally and fight back against the dread incursion of Slaaneshi daemons pouring into their homelands. Were it not for the breakthrough resulting from Teclis' void-quest and the strategic genius of the warlike deity Tyrion, the provinces of Hysh would have been overrun entirely. But through the power of the twin gods, they come back from the brink.

THE REINVENTION
Teclis, having communed with the lunar spirit Celennar and found common ground, learns of how to form a bond with the spirit of an elemental entity. He takes this knowledge back to his people and teaches the most gifted of his mages the art of speaking with the lands. Each of his disciples goes forth into Hysh and takes a new master – not Teclis but one of the major features of the landscape itself. The aelementiri temples of the river, the mountain, the wind and the zenith are formed. Though it takes a lifetime of great sacrifice, those who go to learn at these temples are vested with the power of the lands, rivers and skies above. More than that, their supplications and atonements pacify the angered spirits of Hysh itself, that realmscape that suffered so much over the course of the Ocari Dara. Taking inspiration from these selfless devotees, the rest of Lumineth society reforms, finding their power in the environment around them rather than always

focusing on themselves. A new dawn begins for the Lumineth, and their claim to be masters of the realms is finally borne out.

◉ AGE OF SIGMAR ◉

THE WAY IS BARRED
The lightning of Sigmar's Tempest flashes across Hysh's skies, thunder echoing from the peaks of the Phara'hanya Spine. On columns of pure celestial energy, the Tempest Lords descend, taking the fight to the murderous caravan of Slaaneshi Godseekers known as the Great Vexation that roams the mountain valleys. The Alarith of the Esoteric Peak march out to bar the path of the Stormcast legions, the war forms of a dozen Phara'hanya mountains at their back. The two forces of Order narrowly avoid a costly battle as the Alarith warriors turn aside every Stormcast attack that comes their way without bloodshed, though they do not deign to explain why. Only when a vast, multi-peak avalanche buries much of the Great Vexation does the Lumineth's intent become clear, and the Stormcast and Lumineth fight as one to destroy the survivors. Word of the incident reaches the throne of Sigmar himself. Within a week, a delegation from Azyr has arrived in Xintil, asking for a formal audience with Tyrion and Teclis at their earliest convenience.

BATTLE OF THE SIMULACRA
A flamestorm of daemonic energy summoned by the Black Phoenicians – an Arcanite cult hidden within Xintil's universities – crosses the Girdlesea to reach the Coast of Lucid Dreams. It causes untold havoc, burning and mutating much of the coastlands. When the inferno reaches the lands north of Tor Qulian, it traverses a stretch of land scarred by one of the great disasters of the Ocari Dara – and reopens an old wound in reality. Hundreds of Tzeentchian Flamers spill through, and the firestorm intensifies.

Iliatha's matriarchs have already moved to counter the evil storm, and the forces of that Great Nation surround and contain the daemonic incursion with

uncanny efficiency. Protected from the warpfire by mystical barriers, they close in to engage the foe in combat, and the Flamer daemons are systematically cut down. Yet the minions of Tzeentch have one last trick to play. A strange quirk of the Phoenicians' summoning ritual means that every time one of the daemons is killed, it reforms on the far side of the Realmgate in the Realm of Chaos, ready to plunge through again.

The Clone-Matriarch of Iliatha realises this when she sees the same gangling monstrosity being slain and then reappearing three times in as many hours. She orders a determined counter-assault. Led by a wedge of Dawnriders and the matriarchs themselves, the Auralan infantry press towards the tear in reality at the heart of the flamestorm. One of each pair of clone-twins is ordered through into the hideous, mind-bending landscape of crystal that stretches beyond, whilst the other twin remains behind to continue the fight. So strong is their soul-link that they can still feel each other's minds across the span of the dimensions; when a clone-twin deals a death blow to one of the Flamers in Hysh, their opposite number in the Realm of Chaos destroys the replacement with an uncanny synchronicity that sees the magical rite of reincarnation broken. Though the danger to Iliatha is contained through a triumph of bravery and magical skill, and the rift is sealed with the counter-rite known as the Ceylian Stormbreak, the engagement ends in tragedy – the clone-twins that ventured into the Realm of Chaos find themselves unable to return.

THE GIFT OF SYAR
The Syari Magocracy mounts a retrieval mission into Ulgu when the good-natured ambassador Calenthralle of Naio fails to answer the third magical summons in a row. It is troubling indeed that contact has been lost, for Calenthralle is a zenithal aelementiri, known for translocating above the clouds whenever he feels himself in peril and descending to safety after the danger has passed. Some fear

his disappearance could be the beginning of a realm war if handled poorly, for he is beloved amongst those of the zenith temples. The Syari send a delegation of sages, pathfinders and puzzle-solvers protected by an escort of Auralan warriors to rescue him. In the Cloying Forest, they are attacked by shadow daemons in the employ of Malerion, and they quickly find themselves outnumbered many times over. The Syari escape with their lives – but only just – and are forced to leave behind the treasures and artisan-crafted jewellery they brought with them as ambassadorial gifts.

The darksome daemons that attacked them take the spoils of conquest back to their lairs. There, in the pitch-black catacombs, Calenthralle languishes half-dead after being pitilessly interrogated, bound in tentacular chains of magical shadow to prevent him from translocating to safety. Goaded by the ambassador's claims that one of the artefacts will convey ultimate power, the creatures fight amongst themselves as to who should claim a beautiful brooch that contains a tiny working model of the cosmos.

When the artefact's container is broken in the scuffle, the raw magic of Hysh streams out in such measure that it utterly annihilates the shadow daemons. The ambassador himself uses the energy to turn himself into an ethereal angel of light and, in doing so, breaks his bonds. Better yet, the deadly luminescence acts as a beacon for the Syari delegation to track down and rescue the wounded ambassador. He is returned to his temple, though he never pins the crime of his capture on Malerion and his kin – for he believes the accord between Hysh and Ulgu must be maintained at all costs.

THE RIVER RUNS RED
Mogluk's horde of Destruction, ransacking the sprawling lands of Oralunia after bursting from the Kraggstomp Realmgate, finally meets a foe it cannot defeat: thirst. There is little to nothing in the way to drink in the Oralunian Vastness, a situation that the steed-mounted mages have made worse by magically focusing the heat and light of the desert wastes to unbearable levels as they keep pace with the horde. Half the invading army dies of thirst before it reaches a source of water – Ioda, one of the Great Rivers that carves through the heart of Aurathrai. The orruks of Mogluk's horde descend upon the river and plunge into the shallows, quenching their thirst with wild abandon, only to find themselves under attack from not only their aelven pursuers but also the Lumineth who worship on the Ioda's banks. The river aelementiri attack the invading orruk army with quicksilver grace; racing through the horde as if the greenskins were no more mobile than a copse of trees, they leave hundreds of slashed throats in their wake. Much to the surprise of the Lumineth, the orruks fight on amongst the red waters despite their grievous wounds – after all, only the hardiest of Mogluk's horde survived their long march. But when the river itself manifests a war form, leading those of its tributaries in a surging assault, the battle is soon won. Since then, the Ioda has raged twice as fierce, the rusted armour and drowned corpses of the orruks on its riverbed imbuing it with a savage anger that has infected several river temples.

AN ARROW IN A GALE
When the Blue Scribes lead a teeming shoal of Screamers into the skies of Zaitrec, the aelementiri of the Slicing Gale hear their patron wind spirit howling in protest. The temple warriors race across the Zorostramaran Desert after the invading skyshoal, their long-limbed riding beasts bearing them into battle at a breakneck pace so they can launch killing shafts into the swirling sky-ray formations. The Blue Scribes themselves duel the cloud-riding mages of the temples in scintillating explosions of magic that fill the skies.

For a day and a night, daemonic ectoplasm and magical fire drizzle from the skies, yet still the Blue Scribes ride unharmed. Their arcane wards are proof against any arrow – save one. The Slicing Gale itself takes form just as the Tzeentchian daemons fly towards the Well of Epiphanies; though the fox-faced spirit has borne the direst agony, it will not allow that site to be profaned. On a spiralling weave of ribbons, the spirit rises, drawing back its bowstring and loosing a single deadly shaft that darts this way and that. Borne by living winds to circumvent every arcane ward as a snake would slip through the tangled roots of a tree, the arrow strikes Xirat'p in the chest. P'tarix is forced to screech an emergency incantation of stasis to prevent his brother bursting into two Brimstone Horrors and igniting the piles of parchment gathered around them on their speeding Disc. Opening a portal with a mystical gesture, the Scribes flee back to the Crystal Labyrinth, their sky-sharks alongside them. The Slicing Gale gives a cry of laughter before dissipating on the wind.

THE LANCE OF LIGHT

Tril'hallian, a precocious Zaitreci mage no more than nineteen summers old, steals an orb of translocation from his tutors during a long-planned heist. Further compounding his misdeed, he teleports into his father's inner sanctum. There, he takes up the fabled Lance of the Realm's Edge, the heirloom of his dynasty, intending to carry it against the gheists that assail the borders of his father's citadel. A beam of focused Hyshian magic shoots from the lance, boring through the citadel walls, a nearby museum of music, the scaffolding of a statue of Tyrion, a dozen elder ironbarks, a caravan of human traders, the left leg of the raging Mega-Gargant attacking the caravan, the lower slopes of Mount Orovelai, and sixteen gazellachs grazing on the outer plains of Zaitrec before dissipating at the Perimeter Inimical. Tril'hallian replaces the lance on its display stand, translocates home to return the orb, and wanders innocently back to his scholar-hall to rejoin his fellows.

SETHAI'S SCAR

The substance of Hysh begins to crumble away to miasmas of half-light as the ravages of the Ocari Dara are worsened by Nagash's necroquake. These regions are beautiful to behold, but they are emblematic of a time when there will be nothing physical or solid left of Hysh. The Scinari gather in council under Teclis and devise a way to stop the dissolution. By positioning themselves to form a rune sympathetic to a particular region's plight and enacting a grand solar ritual that channels energy into that rune, they burn a miles-long symbol of the Lumineth's ordered magic into the earth, thereby preventing it from crumbling any further.

THE HOSTS MARCH FORTH

With the Arcanum Optimar still raging and the threat of Slaanesh's vengeance disturbing dreams across the Great Nations, the Lumineth of the Teclian nations gather their forces for war. Teclis mentally prepares himself for the worst of all eventualities – that the Chaos God will break the chains of paradox. Debating the matter at length with Celennar, he communes with the magi of the aelementiri temples. They in turn ask the spirits of the river, mountain, wind and zenith for aid. Lord Tyrion cautions his brother against aggravating their allies by effectively invading the realms of humans, aelves and duardin – even if only to save them from corruption and dissolution – but Teclis is convinced that he is right. Accompanied by the avatars of Hysh, the Lumineth of the Teclian nations go forth in great warhosts and work their runes of stability into a hundred locales; in doing so, they earn the enmity of the very peoples they were endeavouring to protect.

THE ART MADE MANIFEST

Since the coming of the Arcanum Optimar, long-held edicts and prohibitions against the wielding of fell magic have been relaxed – and, in some places, repealed. Those who travel towards the Realm's Edge to dispel hostile manifestations of magic for the betterment of all are often given leave to wield the fiercest sorceries of Hysh for their own devices.

There are several spells that all the Great Nations teach, for they are tied to the realms themselves and can be channelled even in the direst hellscapes. One such spell is the Sanctum of Amyntok. The ground splits to form a ritual circle around the mage, and the life force of the realm springs forth in a crackling shield. Based around the rune Yngra, a sigil synonymous with rescue as well as imprisonment, the shield turns baleful spells and projectiles into flashes of blinding light. Likewise, all foremost Lumineth mages learn to summon the Hyshian Twinstones, a spell that conjures two giant crystal teardrops that orbit one another much as Azyrite astromancers claim Hysh orbits Ulgu. These attract the refracted light of Hysh that would otherwise be lost into the aether with every act of spellcasting. Revolving around one another, they glow brighter with each spell cast, forming a reservoir from which the Lumineth can draw greater power. Perhaps the most feared of all the Lumineth's enduring spells, however, is the legacy of the Alarith Stonemages. Known as the Rune of Petrification, the spell is ripped from the crust of the realm underfoot. Any foes who remain too close to this hovering sigil will find their flesh hardening and turning into stone, until soon they are nothing more than lifelike statues.

ARCHMAGE TECLIS AND CELENNAR

First amongst the Lumineth to bring war to the forces of darkness is Teclis, for he knows well the cost of isolationism. With his kindred spirit Celennar – the incarnate soul of Hysh's true moon – at his side, he descends to the field of battle in a blaze of divine moonlight, searing beams of Hyshian magic all around.

The high lord Teclis is known as the Mage God, for he is one with the arcane power of the realms. Some whisper that he has transcended physicality entirely, becoming a being of pure light that retains a humanoid form only to communicate with those lower down on the ladder of enlightenment that bears his name. Many are the legends about Teclis' former lives – that he sacrificed his mortal life to ensure the aelf race survived, that he unbound the vortex of magic at the heart of the world-that-was in order to deny the Chaos Gods, that he alone kept Hysh from being consumed by the deathly power of the Shyish necroquake. He never speaks to the veracity of the dark rumours that surround his past; as he tells his mage disciples, those who have ventured into shadow for the good of all have earned the prerogative of dwelling in the light.

Teclis' arrival in the Mortal Realms saw him desolate and tormented for many years. Only when he and his brother, Tyrion, entrapped Slaanesh and began to extract aelven souls from within the god did the archmage find a new lease of life. That era was beset with doubt and strife, for even the god-mage found the remaking of an entire race beyond his talents – as the strange curse of the Idoneth bears out. But after several other attempts, he struck upon the correct arcane procedure to turn tortured aelven souls into beings not only hale and hearty but luminous. It was only when the seed of pride that blights every Lumineth personality led to the Ocari Dara that Teclis realised that these creations too were imperfect. By then, it was too late.

With the Ten Paradises riven by war, Teclis desperately sought a way to make the Lumineth whole once more. He searched in ever more esoteric places. It was not whilst climbing the Teclamentari that he found his answer; it was far beyond

it, in the dark of the aetheric void. There, Teclis spoke to the spirit of Hysh's true moon, for he reasoned that it would have the detachment needed to offer solutions he would never find in the Mortal Realms.

As little more than an astral projection of his own soul, Teclis pleaded with Celennar for many days and nights. He was rewarded only with silence and doubt. When the lunar body became eclipsed by Ulgu, passing into darkness as it neared the crux point between the Realms of Light and Shadow, Teclis was beset with such despair he contemplated throwing himself into the void, never to return. Yet when the true moon emerged from shadow once more, there stood a strange and wondrous creature. The essence of Celennar had taken form, manifesting as a winged leonine beast with a serene mask in place of its face.

The creature looked deep into Teclis' psyche. Celennar engaged him in long debate, speaking words straight into the archmage's mind in the tongue of ancient Ulthuan – though, in truth, they were not speaking at all. At first, the moon was entirely inscrutable and all but indifferent to the deeds of the Lumineth. That which occurred within the heartland of Hysh was of little import to one who dwelt so far above it. Yet Teclis talked on, speaking of realities already lost to the scourge of Chaos. The being's gently smiling, mask-like face became sorrowful as Teclis told of the tragedies of the people below and how the survival of the

realms themselves hung by a thread. Something beneath the cold logic of his conclusions spoke to the moon-essence. The scars of former apocalypses had wounded Teclis profoundly, and his voice carried a deepness of emotion and conviction that awakened something within Celennar. A deep disquiet had settled within the moon-creature's soul upon hearing the name of one of the Dark Gods in particular: Slaanesh.

Some aspect of the void spirit shivered in revulsion at the mere mention of the god's name. Celennar promised they would travel alongside Teclis into the realmsphere of Hysh, taking physical form and abandoning their spiritual home to leave the true moon of Hysh itself as nothing more than a lifeless orb of rock. A greater calling had been made clear to them, and they would not abandon it. Through the geomantic arts, they could teach Teclis and his kin to live in harmony with Hysh's lands. With that oath, Celennar turned that final glimmer of hope within Teclis' heart into a ray of illumination that would light the path for his entire race.

Since that day, Teclis and Celennar have been all but inseparable. They often commune in silence high above the arcane stratosphere of Hysh, but when they descend, they alter the course of history. It is not uncommon for the duo to lead a vanguard force and strike a telling blow that will change the fate of the realms. Celennar's aura of moonlight inspires nearby aelves to great feats of heroism as Teclis weaves masterpieces of magical artifice. Searing beams of light shoot from the archmage's palms to banish the enemy from existence, white solar flares roil out from his staff to incinerate those close at hand, and nearby allies move at blurring speed to cut the enemy down. For Teclis is a god amongst mages, blessed by the moon, and he is not afraid to show it.

THE LIGHT OF ELTHARION

Appearing as a resplendent suit of armour that is entirely empty but for a shimmering glow, the Light of Eltharion is an echo of a warrior long dead. He fights with the speed of thought and no normal blade can harm him, for though he is a consummate swordsman and inspirational figure, he is made of nothing more tangible than magic.

Eltharion the Grim was once the pride of the aelven race, a warden of their sacred realm and as gifted a leader as he was a warrior. In the final days of the world-that-was, it was he who directly opposed Nagash's resurrection, the event that inadvertently led to the destruction of the aelven race. Matched in an arcane duel against Arkhan the Black, he fell to the Mortarch's withering spell, and his body was turned to dust. Yet something of his legend lingered on – especially in the minds of Tyrion and Teclis, who had marked his sacrifice well.

The legend of Eltharion had abided across the aeons, and his soul – as strong and luminous as it was – still existed in the form of scattered spiritual energy, having never been claimed by Nagash. Through painstaking meditation and fasting that lasted a full month, Teclis identified the particles of that energy. Seated atop the tall Mount Agiluth, he reached out to them with his mind, linking his consciousness to each tiny mote of spirit that had once been Eltharion – for it was Teclis' theory that the energy of a potent soul could not truly be destroyed.

On his travels, Teclis encountered an aelf who bore a striking resemblance to his old friend, and he persuaded him to agree to the forming of a doppelgänger. Using the strange reproductive magic of Iliatha, Teclis created an inert body, tall and strong, for Eltharion's soul to inhabit. It was arrayed in glory, for while journeying through Syar, Teclis had commissioned artefacts to mirror those heirlooms once borne to war by Eltharion – as best as he could recall them. These included a beautiful Fangsword, a talisman redolent with magic and a suit of ornate armour crested by a helm in the Yvressian style. All that remained was for the soul-motes of Eltharion to occupy the body, and Teclis' old friend would be reborn.

Tragedy struck as the glittering echoes of soul energy entered the mortal body Teclis had prepared. The curse that Arkhan had put upon Eltharion had somehow lingered on, and the simulacrum turned to dust as soon as the soul-motes settled within it. Teclis wept, for his mental odyssey had been punishing and it was hard indeed to see his efforts wasted. But as his tears fell on the mountainside, something remarkable happened. The armour of Eltharion, inhabited only by a softly glowing light, slowly got to its feet and saluted him with the Fangsword.

Teclis has tried to fashion new bodies for the Light of Eltharion to inhabit many times since, but every time he tries, the Iliathan constructs crumble to dust. That has not stopped the warden's soul from fighting alongside the Lumineth, however. At times, he even leads their armies, his telepathic commands sounding loud and clear in the minds of those warhosts he takes to battle. His legend has begun anew, and already many savage and terrible warlords have fallen to his darting blade – few can best a master swordsman whose form is made only of magic and gleaming light.

SCINARI CATHALLARS

Cathallars take the intense emotions stored by their kin in spent aetherquartz and burn them into smoke. In times of battle, these psychoactive vapours billow into the enemy's ranks; those touched by them scream and wail, gnashing and tearing at one another in paroxysms of anguish until they are entirely consumed by pain.

The role of Cathallar is one of consummate importance in Lumineth society. It is they who take the emotion stored in aetherquartz by their contemporaries and, in solemn ritual, burn it away in clouds of raw psychological energy. Such is their skill that the Cathallar can channel this emotional by-product into the ranks of the foe, driving them to madness, or even turn it into harmful emanations that can rake an enemy's soul with talons of despair.

The Cathallar is a solemn figure, bedecked in the deep robes of their order and arrayed with relics of sublimation. Haste is not their way, for to act too fast is to risk letting the thrill of action tip their balanced state of mind into an emotional spiral, which could see them give themselves over to sudden impulse. Instead, they move with a slow and measured calm; their motions are almost trance-like, and even their speech is more like a dark hymn than a rushing, scintillating melody.

Each Cathallar typically keeps their hands and feet bare at all times, the better to stay in touch with the geomantic magic of the lands they roam. Effectively, they ground themselves, allowing the landscape to soak up some of the deadly energies they channel. This means that should the swell of emotion from the spent aetherquartz become too severe, they can funnel it through themselves and out into the realm. Flowers wilt and grass blackens around them as they sluice out the intense emotive power that would otherwise drown them in negative energy. Grief, guilt, despair, rage, gnawing angst – all these things and more burn from the bowl-like censer that is the sacred tool of the Cathallar order, darkening the realm around them with the intensity of the spent feelings.

When the Cathallar wishes to weaponise the deep, negative emotions that burn from their aetherquartz bowl, they do so by psychically guiding the smoking residue into the ranks of the enemy. At first, the foe's eyes water and their minds spiral into confusion, but then, as the emotional burn takes hold, they shiver, shake and convulse. Soon, they are raking their own skin, shrieking their lungs out, clawing at their own eyes and even attacking those around them in a fit of blind rage. Even the undead afflicted by the smoke find voice, wailing and chattering as the intensity of their predicament becomes clear to them and they collapse to the ground.

The Cathallar simply observes, detached and calm, as the enemy falls apart before them. It is a matter of scant seconds before the Lumineth soldiery capitalises on the situation, darting in to put the foe out of their misery with dispassionate efficiency.

'The she-lion does not ask her cubs for permission to slay the wolf. Stay out of our way, human, and trust your elders and betters to do what is right.'

- Iiaara the Bleak, Sage of Tor Limina

THE SHINING COMPANIES OF HYSH

The standing armies of the Lumineth are like no other in the Mortal Realms. Not only are they fast of wit and blade, but they also have an innate talent for magic that allows them to wield the energies of light alongside the finely crafted weapons that are their birthright. It is said that to fight them is to fight the rays of the sun itself.

VANARI AURALAN WARDENS

With searing light glaring out from the points of their pike blocks, the Vanari Auralan Wardens move smoothly forwards, occupying the most tactically advantageous points of the battlefield before planting their feet and making ready to receive the charge. Those enemies foolish enough to brave their phalanx defence are soon enough impaled; once slashed free, their bodies fall down to form a bulwark of corpses that grows taller as the battle grinds towards its gory conclusion.

No haste do the Auralan Wardens employ in their bait-and-slay tactics; they simply wait for the enemy to commit, since their fellows tasked with ranged support take a heavy toll on their adversaries. All too often, their foes see a headlong charge as the only option to escape the rain of arrows and magical bolts that would otherwise destroy them piecemeal. Thinking their numerical superiority will carry the day, the enemies of the Lumineth rush towards their lines, only to be confronted by a forest of spears lowered in perfect unison.

The aelves of Hysh learnt the value of unity the hard way – over the course of the Age of Chaos, they stood apart, for which they paid a terrible price. Since the Reinvention, they have striven to put their individual rivalries aside in order to fight as one. Nowhere is this tactic made more clear than in the ranks of the Auralan Wardens, where the Lumineth stand shoulder to shoulder.

The term 'Auralan' means 'luminous host' and has its origins in magic, as with so much of Lumineth society. Each weapon is enchanted, its tip made of sunmetal that has basked in the light of Hysh for centuries at a time. When the Auralan Wardens call out the correct magical phrase, bolstering their power with aetherquartz to ensure its focus, the tips of these spears glow white-hot. They can melt through a thick breastplate as a heated awl would push through a plate of wax. The spear blocks of the Lumineth have learnt to time this ability perfectly – when the enemy is but a hand's breadth from their blades, their speartips glow bright, and those who think their armour will turn aside or break the polearms realise with a heart-wrenching jolt that they have made a fatal mistake.

A phalanx of Auralan Wardens, when fighting in close order, is a truly glorious sight. The concept of camouflage or stealth has long been forsaken by the Vanari order – better to shine brightest of all and dazzle those with the temerity to look directly upon you. Such is the radiance of the Lumineth that when they gather side by side and channel their power as one, they burn with a fierce white light. This formation is known as a shining company.

It is near impossible to draw a bead upon individual aelves when they are lit by this powerful nimbus; a marksman of the free cities or duardin enclaves who peers through a telescope or scrying lens at a formation of Vanari is asking to be blinded by the experience. When the Vanari are called upon by the eldest of their number to use their aetherquartz reserve – usually kept in the form of a jewel on the helm, decorated weaponry or enhanced armour – they shine all the brighter. The tips of their weapons, be they spears, darts or lances, burn with the energy of tiny suns. This radiance is channelled through the staves and shafts of their weapons and reflected by their artfully made robes and armour as if by a suite of mirrors. The resultant effect is to make the Lumineth appear as if they are bright and angelic figures, transcended from the mortal plane entirely to become beings of searing light. Many a primitive foe who has looked upon the Vanari in this state has concluded that to attack them would be the worst of all follies, choosing to take flight instead of risk their wrath. The forces of darkness that oppose them recoil at the burning touch of this Hyshian energy; even those who steel themselves to strike at these numinous creatures can find their vision blurring and their blade points turned aside.

VANARI AURALAN SENTINELS

The Lumineth place a good deal of importance on ranged warfare, for by engaging the foe at a distance, they can prove their superiority over the enemy without getting mired in the slow grind of close melee.

The Auralan Sentinels have made archery an art form, for the bow is seen as a noble weapon in Hysh. Its ability to pierce the skies, glimmer in the sunshine and then arc down to deliver a swift and relatively clean death speaks to something in the Lumineth soul.

Being aelves, the Auralan Sentinels have improved upon the basic tools of archery used by the simpler-minded races, inventing dozens of varieties of bow and an equally impressive spread of arrows. The most successful design has proven to be the triple-stringed arcbow, the curvature and pull of which allows it to be used in two distinct ways. Should the archer wish to send an arrow straight and true, it will strike with impressive killing force, its shaft flexing and counterflexing at speed as it moves through the air to add a degree of punch when it strikes the target. Should the Auralan Sentinels instead wish to strike from afar, they will send their arrows high, lofting them so they curve back down in a graceful trajectory that dips down sharply at the last moment, thereby circumventing the enemy's armour to strike at their most vulnerable point. By using the scryhawks of their unit's High Sentinel, they can even identify and engage enemies at extreme range. With their leader seeing through the eyes of their avian charges, they can deliver a volley of killing darts that plunge downwards as if from the sun itself to pierce the enemy's flesh. The Auralan Sentinels take a fierce sense of pride from their impressive accuracy, and if they can kill the enemy without risk then they will do so, educating those few who survive in the superlative skills of the Lumineth.

VANARI DAWNRIDERS

The shining white cavaliers of the Vanari Dawnriders go to war upon beautiful stallions native to the Xintilian plains. These riders have formed a powerful bond with their steeds, and together they fight as one, each knowing instinctively what the other will do a moment before they do it. The stallions are each given a name, one that is not chosen consciously but sought through inspiration as the rider presses their forehead against that of their horse. Rider and steed will bond as they gallop across the Xintilian wilderness and through the surf of its golden beaches; leaping over the debris of fallen empires and racing along overgrown forest paths, they will be alight with the sheer elation of speed. On the field of battle, that connection between Dawnrider and mount can be the difference between life and death.

When the Vanari ride together, they do so as a blur of glorious light. Experts at traversing even the densest and most tangled environments, they are neither held back by tumbled statuary nor wrong-footed by corpse-strewn battlefields. Inspired by the legends of mythic riders who burned a trail of white fire through endless ranks of skaven during the Age of Myth, they seek to cut down the hordes and teeming hosts of those who stand against them. Riding close so that the magic of their sunmetal lances bathes them in stark white light, they plunge into the ranks of the enemy at full gallop. When they channel the aetherquartz reserve they keep for the direst of combats, the tips of their weapons become superheated with magic and burn right through the bodies of those they impale, sending their remains scattering upon the wind as white-hot cinders. On and on they ride, blazing a white trail through the enemy army before curving around in a tight parabola and plunging in again. It is said that a full formation of Dawnriders can ride down an enemy force that outnumbers them ten times over.

DISCIPLES OF THE MOUNTAIN

The Alarith have devoted their entire lives to the spirituality of the mountain, and their shared existence has endowed them with supernatural abilities. The warriors of the peaks stand immovable, and when they strike, they do so with the might of stone. At their sides walk the war forms of the very mountains they worship.

The soaring mountains of Hysh have a limitless power, for they have stood tall since the very creation of the Mortal Realms and have borne witness to the lessons of the passing aeons. The Lumineth have come to realise this, and since the Reinvention, they have cherished the knowledge that the mountains can impart to them. To be one with the mountain is to exude an unshakeable confidence, to embody a stoicism that can turn aside the ravages of time, and to harness a wisdom that lasts beyond mortality to define the truths of the realms themselves.

During the Age of Chaos, when the Ocari Dara raged and the skies burned, the destructive forces of the Spirefall created fissures in reality that allowed the energies of Chaos to break through. It was Hysh itself that paid the price, and the mountains were no exception. Many were splintered or crumbled, cored by corrupted magma or infected from the inside out with strange curses that turned once peaceful peaks into malevolent and bitter spirits. To travel their valleys was to be buried under landslides, to climb their pathways was to be shucked off and broken upon cruel rocks, to stand in their shadow was to freeze to death. For long centuries, the mountains were seen as places of fear and trepidation, avoided at all costs by the Lumineth who had once sought their lofty heights as a shortcut to enlightenment.

ALARITH STONEMAGES

Only when Teclis returned from his sojourn to begin the Reinvention did the first Alarith mages approach the mountains in supplication. They braved the worst that the angered peaks could throw at them – sometimes literally. They endured or avoided hailstorms of sharp rocks, crashing boulders, deadly mudslides and avalanches of glittering minerals that would grind and crush all but the most fleet of foot beneath their immense weight. A great many of these pioneers died, but some managed to reach the upper peaks, taking nothing with them and enduring only through their own inner fortitude. They sang laments and songs of supplication to the mountains, asking for their forgiveness with all the lyricism and poetry the aelven soul could muster. They made respectful works of art out of interlocking stones, adorning the shoulders of the broken peaks with beautiful decoration just as a celestial rider might plait the mane of a noble Tauralon. As they fasted under the light of Hysh and its moons, their bodies wasted away over time, and many died.

Eventually, the mountains relented. In offering up their entire lives, and seemingly courting their own deaths, the Alarith mages had proven their desire for atonement to be sincere. Algae and moss grew around them where they sat, and creatures crept from the cracks in the rock to bare their throats. The Alarith ate but sparingly of these gifts, for they realised their relationship with the mountain was tenuous. Over time, however, it became stronger and more robust. The way was opened for a spiritual bond between aelf and mountain that blossomed into a full symbiosis. With the mountain's blessing, the Alarith mages became more stoic and enduring than any breed of aelf before or since.

In battle, Alarith Stonemages use their bond with their geomantic patrons to embody the strength and solidity of the mountain. Rather than becoming incorporeal, as is the forte of the zenith temples, they can become hard as granite for a time – and yet still breathe. They can confer this ability on the Alarith Stoneguard around them, draw power from the symbiosis between mage and warrior alike, entomb the enemy in solid rock, and even channel Hysh's power into the Spirits of the Mountain that form their patrons. To see a Stonemage in battle is to witness a soul in perfect balance, whilst around them enemy regiments crumble and break until they are crushed into a bloody mess.

ALARITH STONEGUARD

The warrior ranks of the Alarith are known as the Stoneguard, and it is they who stand sentinel over the mountain temples that form the focal points of their bond with their elemental patron. It is said that the Stoneguard can stand immobile, their feet rooted to the spot, for years or even decades without partaking of food or drink. So deep is their connection with these aelementor sites that all the nourishment they require is provided by the mountain itself. Should a traveller approach one of their temples, the formerly serene aelves entrusted with the site's protection will move smoothly and quickly to block his path, demanding he declare his business and intent. Those whose answers are found wanting will find their path barred for good – and should they press the matter, they will be rendered unconscious with a sharp blow before being carried from the peaks and thrown unceremoniously back into the lowlands whence they came.

To become an Alarith warrior, an aspirant must seek the blessing of the mountain by fasting, enduring the elements upon the most exposed and hostile of peaks, and even running with the avalanche should the mountain test them in such a manner. Then, at the climax of their trials, they must be literally buried alive by the Alarith they seek to emulate. Should they have earned enough favour with the mountain, they will find themselves able to breathe through tiny cracks in the rock, and after a full week under the earth, they will rise again as Alarith. Those who are not truly sincere in their wish to supplicate themselves will be forever buried underground; the flanks of the most irascible Hyshian mountains are dotted with the corpses of such unworthy souls, their spirits taken by the peaks just as they once sought to take from Hysh. Yet those who rise are given a measure of the mountain's power that they train hard to maximise.

When a temple of Alarith warriors adopt their 'mountain stance', they become all but immovable; even the headlong stampede of a herd of rhinoxen will rebound off a group of Stoneguard who have set themselves to repel a charge. In offence, they become more irresistible force than immovable object; their long-hafted hammers, wielded with superb grace and skill, maximise every arcing swing for the most devastating payload of force. A true strike from such a weapon will crack every bone in the target's body. These hammers contain enchanted rock bequeathed to them by the heart of the mountain, and they hit with incredible force to send even heavily armoured foes scattering in disarray.

Some who study the ways of the mountain seek not to emulate the impervious rock that makes up its vast bulk; rather, they wish to mimic the veins of incredibly precious and magical minerals found within. Instead of wielding the traditional stone longhammers of the first Alarith temples, they use diamond-cored pick-hammers, vicious spikes protruding from the sunsteel heads. Wielded correctly, these can punch straight through even the hell-forged plate of a Daemon Prince, discharging a blaze of light that can banish the creature within if the strike is true.

Regardless of the preferred martial style of their temple, the Alarith champions – known as Truestone Seneschals – may choose to wield paired hammers of sedimentary rock instead of a single greathammer. Some of these weapons' strata are taken from layers of magically potent stone laid down over the course of the formation of the realms themselves, others from the fallout of the Spirefall. These contain so much of the peak's slow but potent wrath that, when twinned with the stolid weight of the granite and diamond that form the rest of the enchanted hammers' construction, they strike with bursts of intense magical energy as well as tremendous crushing force.

AVATARS OF THE HYSHIAN PEAKS

Striding with ground-shaking footfalls across the embattled realms come the Spirits of the Mountain. Crafted from the core of the tallest peaks and inhabited by the animus of the mountain itself, they are prehistoric sentiences roused to battle. To see them fight is to witness the slow-burning anger of Hysh made manifest.

For a mountain's soul to abandon its rocky heartland is sacrifice indeed. It speaks to the depth of the relationship between the Alarith Stonemages and their chosen aelementors that the spirit will agree to take a war form and march far from its home, exchanging the peace and contemplation of the slowly passing seasons to join the Lumineth in the crashing tumult of war.

The ritual by which a Spirit of the Mountain is drawn forth is a long and painstaking process. First, the host form must be created – a vast sculpture of realmstone-rich rock that is not so much hewn as shaped by complex Alarith magic. Atop its broad shoulders is a peak sculpted to echo that of the mountain; more than an imitation, it is a tiny ecosystem unto itself, a microcosm of the mountain from which it has been made. Carefully tended Tohnasai trees sprout from the mock peak's flanks in echo of the ancient cloudbark copses that grow on the mountain's scree-covered slopes.

A massive, two-handed hammer is then crafted for the Spirit of the Mountain to wield, a great deal of care lavished upon it so as not to offend the mountain that will eventually wield it. The mask through which the Spirit will perceive the battlefield is sculpted in the likeness of a sacred Ymetrican Longhorn, that rugged alpine beast that is said to be immortal and, therefore, embodies the mountain more than any other creature. Long banners crafted in the Xintilian style are hung from the Spirit of the Mountain's great mantle, each bearing the likeness and runes of the mountain that is to inhabit it. Then, the host form is clad in ensorcelled armour made of sunmetal that has been quenched in the mountain's lakes and waterfalls – though it looks elegant and clean of line, this armour is proof against even the cannonballs of the Ironweld Arsenal.

Last and most critical of all is the animating spirit that will bring the giant construct to life. The mountain must be convinced that the enemy it has been called upon to fight will threaten the fabric of reality – be it directly, in the manner of the servants of darkness, or unwittingly, in the case of the rampaging tribes. The Lumineth, despite being articulate and persuasive in the extreme, must still spend long weeks pleading their case before the mountain – invariably, it is a spirit that takes its time to come to a decision. If the need is dire enough, it will accede to their request, though that which a mountain considers important is often inscrutable. Yet the effort is unquestionably worthwhile. A Spirit of the Mountain is a massively destructive force, each swing of its hammer enough to shatter the skull of a Maw-krusha, and it can send blasts of geomantic energy from its crest to crush the foe from afar. Those with the temerity to chip at the stone of its host form are unceremoniously flattened, whereas more monstrous foes may be met at full charge, the Spirit's horns slamming into enemy monsters with such force that their prey is killed in a single devastating impact.

AVALENOR, THE STONEHEART KING

The being known as Avalenor is animated by the tallest of Ymetrica's Vertiginous Peaks. He is unique amongst the Spirits of the Mountain in that no living soul knows of his origin; he came to the Alarith temples fully formed, having been convinced to fight in the name of civilisation by Celennar, the spirit of Hysh's true moon.

The theory goes that Avalenor is composed entirely of a naturally occurring type of aetherquartz, voluntarily relinquished by the mountain in order to aid in the fight to keep the Realm of Light sacrosanct. Whether this is true or not, it is widely believed that Avalenor has absorbed the illumination of that realm for millennia. This would certainly explain why he glows with power even amidst the darkness of Ulgu.

The twin hammers that this stone colossus takes to battle carry the weight of aeons, despite their relatively lightweight construction. They strike with such thunderous force that they can topple a city wall with a single blow. Known as the Firestealer Hammers,

they channel the intense and freezing temperatures of Avalenor's peak during the worst of winters. Those who are hit by them will turn as lifeless and black as a corpse that has spent a month frostbitten atop the mountain's upper slopes. It is said that though the weapons often glow with the stolen heat and life force of those they slay, their temperature never rises above that of a glacier's icy heart.

However, it is the elder wisdom of Avalenor that is his most potent weapon. This is a being that has stood tall since the realms first formed, hearkened to the music of the spheres since before the aelven deities came to Hysh, and given the benefit of his insight to kings, emperors and gods alike. Those who ask a worthy question will be entrusted with one of the truths that define the cosmos. They may have to wait a while for the answer, for Avalenor is a creature of deliberation and slow certainty, but those with the patience to earn the Stoneheart King's trust will find themselves enlightened for the rest of their living days.

Archmage Teclis leads the Lumineth host to war, the brilliant light of Hysh heralding a spectacular display of magic and dazzling skill that banishes even the terrifying daemons of Khorne.

A LUMINOUS MAJESTY

The Lumineth are impeccably presented, superlatively skilled and possessed of the utmost surety. Their Vanari formations break the enemy even as the aelementiri temples deliver the hammer blow. Here we present a showcase of Lumineth models expertly painted by the 'Eavy Metal team and Design Studio army painters.

The Realm-lords attack bathed in silvery light, scintillating magic glimmering upon the tips of their blades as their elemental allies stand ready in support. To witness them in battle is to know the splendour of Teclis' masterwork.

Archmage Teclis and Celennar, Spirit of Hysh

Avalenor, the Stoneheart King

Scinari Cathallar

The Light of Eltharion

'This far, but no further.' Under the lambent glow of the ethereal moon Leoth, the Light of Eltharion and the Alarith temple of Mount Lunarest blunt the rampage of an orruk horde. A single step more, and the slaughter begins.

Vanari Dawnrider of Ymetrica *Vanari Dawnrider Standard Bearer* *Steedmaster of Iliatha*

High Sentinel with Scryhawk Lantern

Vanari Auralan Sentinels of Ymetrica

High Sentinel with Scryhawk Lantern

A gleaming company of Vanari Dawnriders gallops hard towards the morbid ranks of Nagash's Ossiarch armies, piercing the deathly miasma with the exorcising light of Hysh.

Alarith Stoneguard
Standard Bearer

Alarith Stoneguard with
diamondpick hammer

Truestone Seneschal
of Ymetrica

*A Spirit of the Mountain strides to battle in defence of Ymetrica, its Alarith acolytes adopting the mountain stance
moments before their Chaos-worshipping enemies charge in.*

Truestone Seneschal of Iliatha

Alarith Stonemage of Ymetrica

Alarith Spirit of the Mountain with stoneheart worldhammer

Vanari Auralan Warden

High Warden of Ymetrica

Vanari Auralan Warden

High Warden of Iliatha

Vanari Auralan Warden

High Warden of Zaitrec

The Vanari Auralan Wardens of Ymetrica face down an advancing tide of skaven Plague Monks. With the ratmen driven by a fanatical devotion, dozens will be impaled on Lumineth pikes before they realise they have met their match.

Beneath the Nautil Peaks, an Alarith temple seeks to reclaim the mountain from the Gloomspite Gitz. The greenskins have the aelves surrounded, but in a burst of light, the tide of battle is soon to change.

THE HOST IMMACULATE

The Lumineth Realm-lords are disciplined, talented and determined aelves who are convinced that their methods of war are the only way that reality can be salvaged from the scourge of Chaos. There are dozens of ways to collect a host of Lumineth; this spread offers one such example of a full and coherent army.

When collecting a Warhammer Age of Sigmar army, it's a good idea to have a plan. How you decide which units to include in your Lumineth Realm-lords host might be based on the look of the models, on how you envision them performing during a battle, or on a narrative found in this battletome. There is no single right way to collect your army, only the way you deem best. The goal is the same – to field an Lumineth host with which to save the realms, whatever the cost! Here's how we assembled the collection shown below.

We decided to build this collection around the notion of symmetry, for that is a major part of the Hyshian mindset. We also considered the army from a narrative standpoint so it would better fit with the background of this exciting new force. We liked the idea of having our units with their models in close formation when they deploy and mirrored so that one half is the reflection of the other. To achieve this, we took two of each of the main units of the Lumineth Realm-lords army and enough characters to make them work at full potential.

Our inner Realm-lord demanded that we be the masters of magic, so we took Teclis himself as our general. With his kindred spirit Celennar at his side, he's no slouch in close combat, and we'll want him in the thick of things to take advantage of his Lunar Staff and Storm of Searing White Light spell. Enemies within 18" had better watch out! He also makes the Lumineth around him far harder to kill. We'll usually choose for him to cast four spells automatically with a casting roll of 10, seriously tipping the scales in our favour as soon as our first hero phase.

As we put our collection together, we noticed that it could also be organised into a few of the warscroll battalions featured later in this battletome. Having two of each kind of Vanari infantry, we were already most of the way to an Auralan Legion, and by including a Scinari Cathallar, we completed the battalion. More than that, we now have a way to turn our aetherquartz consumption – which we anticipate being pretty high early on in the battle – into an advantage rather than a disadvantage. The Cathallar is, in many ways, the lynchpin of the force and will be well defended at all times – the Auralan Legion fights best when packed in a close square, and the Cathallar will be right in the centre. To start, we'll use the deadly archers of the Auralan Sentinels and the copious offensive spells available to us to soften up the enemy's elite forces. Any enemy units that can soak up casualties and still make it to our line will be assaulted by our formations of Dawnriders; these cavaliers excel when attacking hordes of warriors and are fast enough to ensure they keep the pressure on the foe. Anything that threatens our flanks will be held fast by our Alarith troops; they are excellent 'anvil' units that can stop an enemy offensive in its tracks. When the monsters come calling, they'll be met by Avalenor and his fellow Spirit of the Mountain. Keeping the Alarith Stonemage within 12" of these behemoths will ensure that they fight at full effect even when badly wounded. If we can protect our characters, the battle will unfold just as Teclis and his fellow Lumineth intended.

1. Archmage Teclis and Celennar
2. The Light of Eltharion
3. Scinari Cathallar
4. Alarith Stonemage
5. Avalenor, the Stoneheart King
6. Alarith Spirit of the Mountain
7. Vanari Auralan Sentinels
8. Vanari Auralan Sentinels
9. Vanari Auralan Wardens
10. Vanari Auralan Wardens
11. Vanari Dawnriders
12. Vanari Dawnriders
13. Alarith Stoneguard
14. Alarith Stoneguard

'Your kind is no longer at liberty to befoul the rightful domain of others. The realms do not wish to be blackened by your filth, neither can the laws of the cosmos abide your hateful presence. We are the blades of the realms, foul beast. On their behalf, we will slay you all.'

- Ylonguile qu Spiriar, Tor Xillion

PAINTING YOUR LUMINETH

A Lumineth Realm-lords army is an exciting painting challenge whether you are a veteran hobbyist or you have never picked up a paintbrush in your life. On the following pages, you will find stage-by-stage guides to help you make the most of your Lumineth Citadel Miniatures, with tips and examples from the experts.

There is nothing like the sight of a fully painted army of Citadel Miniatures, and a magnificent host of Lumineth Realm-lords can be truly breathtaking. There is real satisfaction to be had in adding colour to your collection, teasing out the finely sculpted details, making your miniatures your own and creating a unified force. After all, one painted model looks great, but an entire army brought together through shared colours, iconography and ornate heraldry is even better.

Before painting your models, you'll first need to assemble them. To begin with, we suggest you follow the advice given in the construction booklet provided with your models.

There's no right or wrong way to go about painting your collection of miniatures. Some people revel in treating each miniature as a work of art, lavishing attention on every millimetre of every model and painstakingly crafting scenic bases. Others prefer a far simpler approach with basic but consistent paint jobs that allow them to quickly complete legions of warriors. And, of course, there is plenty of middle ground for those who enjoy painting their troops but want to devote special attention to key figures such as an Alarith Spirit of the Mountain. Again, there is no one way to paint, just the way that works best for you. In the end, the goal is to field a fully painted army of Realm-lords on the tabletop.

On the following pages, you will find stage-by-stage guides, variant colour schemes and top tips to inspire you as you paint your Lumineth host.

WARHAMMER TV

Warhammer TV's painting tutorials have insights for everyone as they show you how to paint Citadel Miniatures from start to finish. The guides are available for free on games-workshop.com and can also be watched via the Warhammer TV YouTube channel. Why not take a moment to check them out?

UNDERCOAT
For the Ymetrica colour scheme, spray your models with Wraithbone. This will give you a bright foundation for the subsequent basecoats and layers of Contrast paint. For best results, follow the instructions on the spray can, and make sure you give it a really good shake!

TOP TIP
It is good practice to apply a coat of Munitorum Varnish spray or Stormshield to your models to protect your paint jobs against the wear and tear of battle.

YMETRICA – ARMOUR

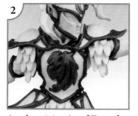

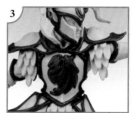

1. Apply two thin coats of Corax White Base paint to the plate armour sections.

2. Apply a 1:1 mix of Dryad Bark and Lahmian Medium to the armour trim and any areas that will later be painted gold.

3. Tidy up with Corax White, then add a highlight of White Scar to any white edges, such as those on the helm.

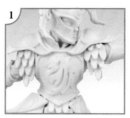

4. Layer the trim with Liberator Gold, avoiding any areas that are going to be ornate gold, such as the insignia on the breastplate.

5. Carefully apply a highlight of Runefang Steel to the edges of the trim.

At this point, any areas that are going to be ornate gold have only been painted with a 1:1 mix of Dryad Bark and Lahmian Medium. Once you are happy with the gold trim, the next stage is to work on these elements, including iconography, gold details on weapons, gem casings and trinkets.

YMETRICA – ORNATE GOLD ELEMENTS

1 Over the Dryad Bark mix mentioned previously, apply Retributor Armour, leaving the recesses dark.

2 Shade with Agrax Earthshade Gloss. You can leave it here for a Battle Ready finish.

3 For an extra level of finish, apply a few thin coats of Liberator Gold to the raised areas.

4 Paint the most prominent edges of the symbol or ornate area with Runefang Steel.

YMETRICA – CLOTH

1 If you need to tidy up the cloth areas, do so with Wraithbone Base paint.

2 Apply a 1:1 mix of Skeleton Horde and Contrast Medium for a Battle Ready finish.

3 For an extra level of finish, highlight the creases of the cloth with Wraithbone.

4 Finally, carefully paint the trim of the cloth with White Scar.

YMETRICA – SCALE MAIL AND BLADES

 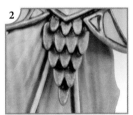 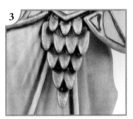 

1 Apply a basecoat of Grey Knights Steel.

2 Apply a shade of Nuln Oil Gloss. You can leave it here for a Battle Ready finish.

3 For more definition, add a highlight of Runefang Steel.

Paint your blades using the same method. Apply fine lines of Runefang Steel to the edges.

YMETRICA – UNDERSKIRT

 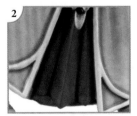 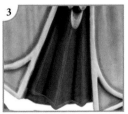 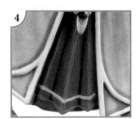

1 Apply a basecoat of Alaitoc Blue.

2 Shade the recesses with Ultramarine Blue Contrast paint.

3 Highlight the edges of the underskirt with Hoeth Blue.

4 If you have a steady hand, carefully paint a horizontal line of Corax White near the bottom of the underskirt.

YMETRICA - CREST

1 Apply a basecoat of Hoeth Blue over a Wraithbone undercoat.

2 Carefully paint broad stripes on the plumes with Kantor Blue.

3 Edge highlight the light blue areas with lines of Celestra Grey.

4 Edge highlight the dark blue areas with Hoeth Blue. Follow the steps for ornate gold to paint the gold ovals.

YMETRICA - SHIELD

 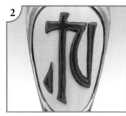 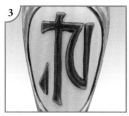 

1 Apply a basecoat of Kantor Blue to the rune. You may need to tidy up with Corax White afterwards.

2 Edge highlight the rune with Alaitoc Blue.

3 For additional contrast, apply Lothern Blue to the corners of the design.

On the back of the shield, apply Cygor Brown, then drybrush with Karak Stone.

PALE SKIN

EYES & TEETH

HAIR

1 Over a Wraithbone undercoat, apply a 1:1 mix of Guilliman Flesh and Contrast Medium.

2 Apply a couple of thin coats of Flayed One Flesh to the raised areas of skin.

Apply Wyldwood to the recesses of the teeth and eyes. Paint the teeth and the whites of the eyes with White Scar, then dot the eyes with Macragge Blue.

Base: Ungor Flesh.
Shade: Seraphim Sepia.
Highlight: Screaming Skull.

AURALAN BOW

 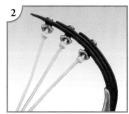 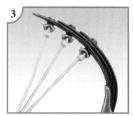 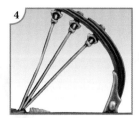

1 Apply a Doombull Brown basecoat.

2 Shade with Nuln Oil, focusing on the recesses.

3 Edge highlight with Baneblade Brown.

4 Apply a coat of Basilicanum Grey to the strings.

DETAILS

Scabbard: Basecoat with Doombull Brown, shade the recesses with Agrax Earthshade and highlight with Skrag Brown.

Gloves: Over Dryad Bark, shade the recesses with Nuln Oil, then highlight with Gorthor Brown and Baneblade Brown.

AETHERQUARTZ GEMS

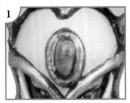

1

Over a Grey Seer basecoat, apply a 1:1 mix of Volupus Pink and Contrast Medium.

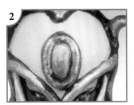

2

Apply a few thin coats of White Scar to the top half of the gem, creating a gradual transition from dark to light.

STALLIONS

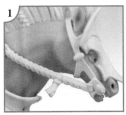

1

Undercoat the stallions (but not the riders) with Corax White spray. Then, apply a basecoat of Kislev Flesh to the skin.

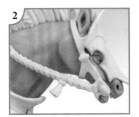

2

Shade the stallion's skin with a 1:2 mix of Skeleton Horde and Contrast Medium.

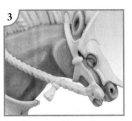

3

Apply some thinned highlights of Screaming Skull to the raised edges of the skin.

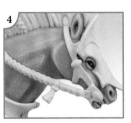

4

Apply Abaddon Black to the eyes and dot with White Scar. Paint the teeth with Rhinox Hide and line with Corax White.

STALLION DETAILS

Mane: Basecoat with Wraithbone, add a coat of Skeleton Horde and then highlight with Wraithbone.

Hooves: Basecoat with Dryad Bark, then highlight with Gorthor Brown. Apply Karak Stone to the edges of the hoof.

Socks: You can paint a variety of patterns on your stallion's socks. We've used Wraithbone and Skeleton Horde, as with the mane.

Tassels: Basecoat with Teclis Blue, shade with Drakenhof Nightshade and then highlight with Hoeth Blue.

DETAILS

Leaves: Basecoat with Elysian Green, shade with Biel-Tan Green, highlight with Ogryn Camo.
Wood: Basecoat with Mournfang Brown, shade with Agrax Earthshade, Skrag Brown highlights.

Lantern: Basecoat with Pink Horror and then carefully shade the recesses with thinned Daemonette Hide. Highlight with Emperor's Children and Fulgrim Pink.

Glowing Cracks: Shade the recesses with Black Templar. To create a glowing energy effect, paint with thinned Caledor Sky followed by Teclis Blue, then add dots of White Scar.

Cathallar Robes: Basecoat with Night Lords Blue and shade with Nuln Oil. Highlight the raised edges of the cloth with Kantor Blue and Alaitoc Blue. Pick out the most prominent areas with Hoeth Blue.

SHEER VEIL

Undercoat the model with Wraithbone spray. Apply a 1:2 mix of Guilliman Flesh and Contrast Medium to the face.

Then, apply two thin coats of Hoeth Blue to the veil. Be careful not to go too far on to the face, as we want this area to stay light.

Carefully layer Fenrisian Grey on the raised areas of the veil and the folds across the face to create the effect of sheer material.

Finally, apply thin coats of Fenrisian Grey as a soft highlight on the raised areas of the veil and the folds covering the face.

PSYCHOACTIVE SMOKE

Apply a basecoat of Abaddon Black to the smoke plumes.

Next, layer with Night Lords Blue, avoiding the recesses.

Add Alaitoc Blue highlights to the areas painted Night Lords Blue.

Apply a fine highlight and a few speckles of Fenrisian Grey to finish.

ALARITH DETAILS

Robe: Basecoat with Grey Seer, then apply an all-over 1:3 mix of Basilicanum Grey and Contrast Medium. Highlight with Grey Seer and paint the trim with Corax White.

Hammer: Basecoat the rock with Mechanicus Standard Grey, then shade with Agrax Earthshade. Highlight with Dawnstone.

Diamondpick: Create hints of colour by thinning Emperor's Children, Yriel Yellow and Teclis Blue with Lahmian Medium until the hues are nearly transparent.

Armour: Over a Corax White undercoat, use a 1:8 mix of Dryad Bark and Lahmian Medium to pick out the patterns, followed by a soft drybrush of Grey Seer over the top.

Mountains: Over a Grey Seer basecoat, apply a coat of Basilicanum Grey. Drybrush with Dawnstone and Administratum Grey.

Fur: Basecoat with Skavenblight Dinge and apply a shade of Agrax Earthshade. Highlight with Stormvermin Fur and Karak Stone.

Hammer Cracks: Add Caledor Sky and thinned Temple Guard Blue to the recesses. Add spots of White Scar to intensify the glow.

ZAITREC - ARMOUR, CLOTH AND DETAILS

1
Apply two thin coats of Retributor Armour as a basecoat.

2
Add an all-over shade of Agrax Earthshade Gloss. You can leave it here for a Battle Ready finish.

3
For an extra level of finish, layer the armour with Liberator Gold.

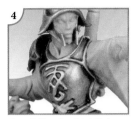

4
Carefully edge highlight with Runefang Steel.

Banner: Basecoat with Grey Seer. Add a coat of Apothecary White, then layer with Corax White.

Trim: Apply a basecoat of Screamer Pink, then highlight with Pink Horror.

Crest: Follow the steps for the banner and trim to create the white and magenta stripes.

Rune: Basecoat with Ironbreaker, shade with Nuln Oil Gloss, highlight with Stormhost Silver.

ILIATHA - ARMOUR, CLOTH AND DETAILS

1
Undercoat the model with Corax White spray, then consider making an exact copy of the model to be their clone-twin!

2
Next, shade the recesses with a 1:1 mix of Drakenhof Nightshade and Lahmian Medium. Tidy up with a little Corax White if needed.

Cloth: Over a Corax White undercoat, apply Gryph-hound Orange and Jokaero Orange, then add Kislev Flesh highlights. Paint the trim with Corax White.

Underskirt: Basecoat with Khorne Red, then shade the recesses with Nuln Oil. Edge highlight with Wazdakka Red and Cadian Fleshtone.

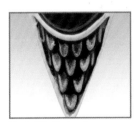

Scale Mail: Apply a basecoat of Castellax Bronze, then shade with Agrax Earthshade Gloss. Edge highlight with Runefang Steel.

Crest: Basecoat with Khorne Red, then apply an all-over shade of Nuln Oil. Highlight with Mephiston Red and Jokaero Orange.

Chest Icon: Basecoat with Khorne Red, then shade the recesses with Nuln Oil. Add edge highlights of Evil Sunz Scarlet and Fire Dragon Bright.

Rune: Apply a basecoat of Runelord Brass and shade with Agrax Earthshade. Layer with Sycorax Bronze and edge highlight with Runefang Steel.

YMETRICA VARIANT – ARMOUR, CLOTH AND DETAILS

Armour: Over a basecoat of Ironbreaker, apply a 1:3 mix of Akhelian Green and Contrast Medium. Then, highlight with Ironbreaker.

Shield Field: Basecoat with Kantor Blue, shade the recesses with Nuln Oil and add edge highlights of Alaitoc Blue and Teclis Blue.

Crest: Over a basecoat of Grey Seer, apply a 1:2 mix of Talassar Blue and Contrast Medium. Then, highlight with Blue Horror.

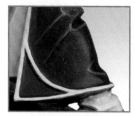

Robe: Basecoat with Night Lords Blue, then layer with Kantor Blue. Highlight with Alaitoc Blue and Teclis Blue. Paint the trim with Corax White.

Underskirt: Basecoat with Lothern Blue, then shade the recesses with a 1:1 mix of Drakenhof Nightshade and Lahmian Medium. Edge highlight with Blue Horror.

Rune: Apply a basecoat of Retributor Armour, then shade with Reikland Fleshshade Gloss. Edge highlight with Runefang Steel.

Boots: Basecoat with Rakarth Flesh, then shade the recesses with Agrax Earthshade. Layer with Pallid Wych Flesh, leaving the recesses dark.

Bow Limbs: Basecoat with Corax White. Apply Gryph-charger Grey to the recesses. Tidy with Corax White as needed.

STALLION VARIANTS

Skin: Basecoat with Grey Seer and apply an all-over 1:2 mix of Gryph-charger Grey and Contrast Medium. Highlight with Grey Seer. You can stipple areas with Gryph-charger Grey to add patterns to the skin.

Mane: Basecoat with Corvus Black. Highlight with Stormvermin Fur and Karak Stone.

Skin: Basecoat with Wraithbone and apply an all-over 1:1 mix of Skeleton Horde and Contrast Medium. Highlight with Screaming Skull and Wraithbone. You can stipple on patterns with Skeleton Horde.

Mane: Basecoat with Dryad Bark. Highlight with Skrag Brown and Tau Light Ochre.

Skin: Basecoat with Grey Seer and apply an all-over 1:3 mix of Basilicanum Grey and Contrast Medium. Highlight with Grey Seer.

Mane: Basecoat with Karak Stone and shade with Agrax Earthshade. Then, highlight with Ushabti Bone and Screaming Skull.

LUMINETH BASING

Hyshian Grasslands: Apply Stirland Mud to the base and wait for it to completely dry. Then, apply a heavy drybrush of Deathclaw Brown and finish off with a lighter drybrush of Screaming Skull. Add some Middenland Tufts and Mordheim Turf to create your grasslands.

Snowy Tundra: Apply Stirland Battlemire to the base. Once dry, drybrush with Mournfang Brown and Morghast Bone. Add some Middenland Tufts and patches of Valhallan Blizzard, using the tip of your brush to gently add snow to the tufts.

Arid Wasteland: Cover the base with areas of Armageddon Dust and Agrellan Earth. Shade with Agrax Earthshade, then drybrush with Morghast Bone. Apply the smallest tufts of Mordheim Turf sparingly. **TOP TIP:** Use clippers to divide large clumps into smaller tufts.

Fallen Empire: Using a Shattered Dominion base, apply Mournfang Brown to the cracks, then drybrush with Balor Brown and Screaming Skull. Paint the stone by following the masonry guide below. For the crystal rocks, basecoat with Grey Seer, apply a coat of Akhelian Green and highlight with Grey Seer.

White Stone: Basecoat a Shattered Dominion base with Grey Seer. Next, apply a coat of Apothecary White followed by a drybrush of White Scar. Apply Gryph-charger Grey to the rocks and raised detailing of your choice. Finally, add the smallest Middenland Tufts sparingly.

Spell-cursed Wastes: Apply Grey Seer and Talassar Blue to the base. Add a thick coat of Mordant Earth and leave to dry. Paint the Barbed Bracken with Caledor Sky, Teclis Blue and White Scar, working inwards to create a glowing effect. **TOP TIP:** Paint the rim of the base Steel Legion Drab.

MASONRY

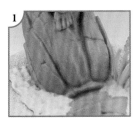
1

Over a Wraithbone undercoat, basecoat with Karak Stone to create a neutral stone effect.

2

Apply an all-over 1:1 mix of Space Wolves Grey and Contrast Medium.

3

Drybrush with Grey Seer, taking care to catch the edges of the bas-relief design.

WHEAT

Base: Ogryn Camo.
Shade: Seraphim Sepia.
Highlight: Screaming Skull.

THE ARMIES OF THE REALM-LORDS

This battletome contains all of the rules you need to field your Lumineth Realm-lords miniatures on the battlefields of the Mortal Realms, from a host of exciting allegiance abilities to a range of warscrolls and warscroll battalions. The rules are split into the following sections:

ALLEGIANCE ABILITIES

This section describes the allegiance abilities available to a Lumineth Realm-lords army. The rules for using allegiance abilities can be found in the *Warhammer Age of Sigmar Core Book*.

BATTLE TRAITS

Abilities available to every unit in a Lumineth Realm-lords army (pg 65), as well as those specific to **VANARI** and **ALARITH** units (pg 66-67).

COMMAND TRAITS

Abilities available to the general of a Lumineth Realm-lords army if it is a **SCINARI** or **ALARITH HERO** (pg 66-67).

ARTEFACTS OF POWER

Artefacts available to **SCINARI** and **ALARITH HEROES** in a Lumineth Realm-lords army (pg 66-67).

SPELL LORES

Spells available to **WIZARDS** in a Lumineth Realm-lords army (pg 68-69).

GREAT NATIONS

Abilities for four of the Great Nations of Hysh (pg 70-73). These rules can be used by units in a Lumineth Realm-lords army that have been given the appropriate keyword (see the Lumineth Great Nations battle trait, opposite).

BATTLEPLANS

This section includes two new narrative battleplans (pg 74-77) that can be played with a Lumineth Realm-lords army.

PATH TO GLORY

This section contains rules for using your Lumineth Realm-lords collection in Path to Glory campaigns (pg 78-81).

WARSCROLLS

This section includes all of the warscrolls you will need to play games of Warhammer Age of Sigmar with your Lumineth Realm-lords miniatures. There are three types of warscroll included in this section:

WARSCROLL BATTALIONS

These are formations made up of several Lumineth Realm-lords units that combine their strengths to gain powerful new abilities (pg 82-83).

WARSCROLLS

A warscroll for each unit is included here. The rules for using a Lumineth Realm-lords unit, along with its characteristics and abilities, are detailed on its warscroll (pg 84-92).

ENDLESS SPELL WARSCROLLS

There are three endless spell warscrolls that detail the rules for unique and powerful spells that can be summoned by **LUMINETH REALM-LORDS WIZARDS** (pg 94-95). The rules for playing games with endless spells can be found in the *Warhammer Age of Sigmar Core Book* and in *Warhammer Age of Sigmar: Malign Sorcery*.

PITCHED BATTLE PROFILES

This section contains Pitched Battle profiles for the units, warscroll battalions and endless spells in this book (pg 96).

ALLIES

This section has a list of the allies a Lumineth Realm-lords army can include (pg 96).

ALLEGIANCE ABILITIES
LUMINETH REALM-LORDS

BATTLE TRAITS – POWER OF THE LUMINETH

AETHERQUARTZ RESERVE
Every Lumineth Realm-lord carries with them a tiny reserve of aetherquartz that they keep in a gem-like container. In extremis, the Realm-lord can break the vessel's seal, allowing them to temporarily increase their physical and arcane prowess, albeit at a heavy emotional cost.

Each unit in a Lumineth Realm-lords army starts the battle with 1 aetherquartz reserve. Once per phase, you can say that 1 unit will use its aetherquartz reserve to use 1 of the following aetherquartz reserve abilities. However, if you do so, subtract 1 from that unit's Bravery characteristic for the rest of the battle.

Heightened Reflexes: You can say that a unit will use this ability when it is picked to be the target of an enemy attack. If you do so, add 1 to save rolls for attacks that target that unit until the end of that phase.

Heightened Senses: You can say that a unit will use this ability when it is picked to shoot or fight. If you do so, add 1 to hit rolls for attacks made by that unit until the end of that phase.

Magical Boost: You can say that a unit will use this ability after it has attempted to cast a spell but before any unbinding rolls are made for that spell. If you do so, you can either add 1 to that casting roll or re-roll that casting roll.

Magical Insight: You can say that a unit will use this ability at the start of your hero phase. If you do so, that unit can attempt to cast 1 extra spell in that phase.

ABSORB DESPAIR
Scinari Cathallars can assuage the dark despair that afflicts a Lumineth Realm-lord after the use of their aetherquartz reserve. The negative energies are not just burned off but released towards the foe as a psychological weapon.

If a friendly unit uses its aetherquartz reserve while it is wholly within 18" of any friendly **CATHALLARS**, you can pick 1 of the **CATHALLARS** within 18" of that unit and say that they will absorb the negative energy. A **CATHALLAR** cannot absorb negative energy more than once per phase.

If a **CATHALLAR** absorbs the negative energy from a friendly unit, do not subtract 1 from that unit's Bravery characteristic. Instead, you can pick 1 enemy unit within 18" of that **CATHALLAR**. If you do so, subtract 1 from the Bravery characteristic of that enemy unit for the rest of the battle. The same enemy unit cannot be affected by this ability more than once per battle.

LIGHTNING REACTIONS
Lumineth Realm-lords possess a natural skill and talent that far outstrips that of most other races. When combined with decades of martial training, this creates a warrior elite that can think faster, act more decisively and fight more proficiently than any other.

During the combat phase, when it is your turn to pick a unit to fight, you can pick 2 eligible units instead of 1. If you do so, each of those units can fight one after the other in the order of your choice.

Designer's Note: *This ability only applies to units that fight during the combat phase; therefore, it cannot be used for units that fight at the start or the end of the combat phase, or for units that fight in any phase other than the combat phase.*

LUMINETH GREAT NATIONS
The Lumineth are gathered into Great Nations, each with their own unique culture, specialisations and sets of social mores.

When you choose an Lumineth Realm-lords army, you can give it a Great Nation keyword from the list below. All **LUMINETH REALM-LORDS** units in your army gain that keyword, and you can use the allegiance abilities listed for that Great Nation on the page indicated.

- **YMETRICA** (pg 70)
- **SYAR** (pg 71)
- **ILIATHA** (pg 72)
- **ZAITREC** (pg 73)

If a model already has a Great Nation keyword on its warscroll, it cannot gain another one. This does not preclude you from including the unit in your army, but you cannot use the allegiance abilities for its Great Nation.

VANARI

BATTLE TRAITS – WARRIORS OF LIGHT

SHINING COMPANY
Vanari warriors often fight in a tight grouping, so close that their shoulders or stirrups are almost touching. This densely packed formation sacrifices a little fluidity but combines the bright light of each numinous soul into a dazzling brilliance that befuddles enemies.

After a **VANARI** unit is set up, if the base of each model in the unit is touching the bases of 2 or more other models from the same unit, then that unit becomes a shining company.

That unit remains a shining company until, after finishing a move, the base of each model in the unit is no longer touching the bases of 2 or more other models from the same unit, or until, after removing a slain model from the unit, the bases of any remaining models in the unit are not touching the bases of 2 or more other models from the same unit.

Subtract 1 from hit rolls for attacks that target a shining company. However, a shining company cannot run or charge, and models in that unit can only move 1" when they pile in.

SCINARI

COMMAND TRAITS – LORDS OF BRILLIANCE
CATHALLAR generals only.

D3 Command Trait

1 Spellmaster: *This general has studied the arcane arts for centuries.*

Once in each of your hero phases, you can re-roll 1 failed casting roll for this general.

2 Loremaster: *Few can rival this general's knowledge of aelven magic.*

This general knows 1 extra spell from the Lore of Hysh (pg 68).

3 Warmaster: *This general has mastered advanced strategies and tactics of battle.*

If this general is part of your army and on the battlefield at the start of your hero phase, roll a dice. On a 4+, you receive 1 extra command point.

ARTEFACTS OF POWER – HEIRLOOMS OF HYSH
CATHALLARS only.

D3 Artefact of Power

1 Phoenix Stone: *This ancient crystal can heal those on the brink of death.*

If a friendly **LUMINETH REALM-LORDS HERO** is slain within 12" of the bearer, before removing that model from play, roll a dice. On a 6, that model is not slain, all wounds allocated to it are healed and any wounds that currently remain to be allocated to it or its unit are negated.

2 Silver Wand: *This slender wand is covered with winding Lumineth runes.*

The bearer can attempt to cast 1 extra spell in your hero phase.

3 Blade of Leaping Gold: *A more finely balanced blade than this has never been wrought.*

Pick 1 of the bearer's melee weapons. Add 3 to the Attacks characteristic of that weapon.

ALARITH

BATTLE TRAITS - MOUNTAIN KINDRED

ENDURING AS ROCK

When in a battle trance inspired by the mountain, the Alarith take on the aspect of stone, blades rebounding off their rock-hard skin.

After armies have been set up but before the first battle round begins, and at the start of any of your hero phases, you can pick any number of friendly **ALARITH** units and say that they are adopting the mountain stance. If you do so, until your next hero phase, if the weapon used for an attack that targets an **ALARITH** unit in the mountain stance has a Rend characteristic of -1, change the Rend characteristic for that attack to '-'.

TECTONIC FORCE

The Alarith are imbued with the grinding, unstoppable power of the tectonic plates that created the mountains of Hysh.

At the end of each combat phase, you can pick 1 enemy unit within 1" of each friendly **ALARITH** unit. You cannot pick the same enemy units more than once in the same phase. After you pick each unit, your opponent must move that unit 2" and that unit must finish that move more than 1" from any **ALARITH** units from your army if it is possible for it to do so.

Once those enemy units have been forced to move, any friendly **ALARITH** units that are within 3" of any enemy units can make a 1" pile-in move.

COMMAND TRAITS - LORDS OF STONE
ALARITH generals only.

D3 Command Trait

1 **Majestic:** *Few can look upon this general and not be awed by their luminous majesty.*

Add 1 to the Bravery characteristic of friendly **LUMINETH REALM-LORDS** units while they are wholly within 12" of this general. In addition, subtract 1 from the Bravery characteristic of enemy units while they are within 18" of this general.

2 **Enduring:** *This general's stamina is legendary.*

Add 3 to this general's Wounds characteristic.

3 **Loremaster:** *Few can rival this general's knowledge of aelven magic.*

If this general is a **WIZARD**, they know 1 extra spell from the Lore of the High Peaks (pg 69).

ARTEFACTS OF POWER - GIFTS OF THE MOUNTAINS
ALARITH HEROES only.

D3 Artefact of Power

1 **Heartstone Amulet:** *This fragment of mountain heartstone lends the bearer an indomitable toughness.*

Roll a dice each time you allocate a wound or mortal wound to the bearer. On a 5+, that wound or mortal wound is negated.

2 **Ebony Stone:** *Dark as midnight jet, this rock absorbs the arcane energy of hostile spells.*

Each time the bearer is affected by a spell or endless spell, you can roll a dice. On a 4+, ignore the effects of that spell on the bearer.

3 **Magmic Hammer:** *This volcanic hammer shimmers red-hot as it unleashes powerful arcane bolts.*

If the bearer is a **WIZARD**, add 1 to the number of mortal wounds inflicted by Arcane Bolt spells that are cast by the bearer.

SPELL LORES

You can choose or roll for one spell from one of the following tables for each **Wizard** in a Lumineth Realm-lords army. **Teclis** knows all of the spells in all of the following tables.

LORE OF HYSH

Teclis, Light of Eltharion, Cathallars and **Vanari Wizards** only.

D6	Spell

1   Speed of Hysh: *The caster gestures at a nearby Lumineth regiment, enchanting them so they can move blurringly fast.*

Speed of Hysh has a casting value of 5. If successfully cast, pick 1 friendly **Lumineth Realm-lords** unit wholly within 18" of the caster and visible to them. Double the Move characteristic of that unit until your next hero phase.

2   Solar Flare: *Communing with the solar bodies above the battlefield, the caster causes one of them to belch forth a searing flare of energy that disrupts the magical energy across the battlefield.*

Solar Flare has a casting value of 8. If successfully cast, pick a point on the battlefield within 10" of the caster and visible to them. If there is an endless spell at that point, it is dispelled, and if there is a unit at that point, roll a number of dice equal to the number of models in that unit. For each 6+, that unit suffers 1 mortal wound. In addition, until your next hero phase, subtract 2 from casting, dispelling and unbinding rolls for **Wizards** within 12" of that point.

3   Lambent Light: *The wizard points at a foe and calls down a ghostly illumination that makes them starkly visible to their enemies.*

Lambent Light has a casting value of 5. If successfully cast, pick 1 enemy unit within 18" of the caster and visible to them. Until your next hero phase, you can re-roll hit rolls for attacks made with missile weapons that target that unit.

4   Ethereal Blessing: *By focusing their will and concentrating deeply, the caster makes an ally as insubstantial as the light of the moon.*

Ethereal Blessing has a casting value of 6. If successfully cast, pick 1 friendly **Lumineth Realm-lords** unit wholly within 18" of the caster and visible to them. Until your next hero phase, ignore modifiers (positive or negative) when making save rolls for attacks that target that unit.

5   Total Eclipse: *The caster gestures towards a lunar body above their head, causing a dark shadow to draw across it. This distracts the foe and makes it hard for their leaders to issue effective commands.*

Total Eclipse has a casting value of 8. If successfully cast, until your next hero phase, your opponent must spend 2 command points to use a command ability instead of 1.

6   Protection of Hysh: *The caster opens their arms wide, creating a field of glowing energy that protects all of the caster's allies that are nearby.*

Protection of Hysh has a casting value of 8. If successfully cast, until your next hero phase, roll a dice each time you allocate a wound or mortal wound to a friendly unit wholly within 9" of the caster. On a 5+, that wound or mortal wound is negated. This spell cannot be cast in the same hero phase as Protection of Teclis.

LORE OF THE HIGH PEAKS
Teclis and **Alarith Wizards** only.

D6   Spell

1   **Unyielding Calm:** *The caster imbues an ally with the unbreakable stoicism of the mountains.*

Unyielding Calm has a casting value of 4. If successfully cast, pick 1 friendly **Lumineth Realm-lords** unit wholly within 18" of the caster. Until your next hero phase, do not take battleshock tests for that unit.

2   **Crippling Vertigo:** *The caster visualises standing upon a narrow ledge of a high mountain and transfers this image into the minds of their foes, amplifying it until it consumes them entirely.*

Crippling Vertigo has a casting value of 6. If successfully cast, pick 1 enemy unit wholly within 18" of the caster and visible to them. Until your next hero phase, roll 2D6 before that unit makes a normal move, a charge move or a pile-in move. If the roll is greater than that unit's Bravery characteristic, it cannot make that move.

3   **Voice of the Mountains:** *The caster communes with a nearby peak, his war shout growing ever louder into a thunderous rumble of stone that fills the foe with dread before eventually fading.*

Voice of the Mountains has a casting value of 6. If successfully cast, until the end of the turn, subtract 2 from the Bravery characteristic of enemy units. Then, until your next hero phase, subtract 1 from the Bravery characteristic of enemy units instead.

4   **Living Fissure:** *The caster touches a rocky outcrop, causing it to split apart along its entire length.*

Living Fissure has a casting value of 6. If successfully cast, pick 1 point on the battlefield within 9" of the caster that is visible to them and draw an imaginary straight line 1mm wide between that point and the closest part of the caster's base. Roll a dice for each unit that has models passed across by this line. On a 2+, that unit suffers D3 mortal wounds.

5   **Entomb:** *The caster points at a foe and closes their hand into a tight fist. The ground opens beneath their victim, engulfing them in a prison made of solid rock.*

Entomb has a casting value of 7. If successfully cast, pick 1 enemy model within 18" of the caster and visible to them, and roll a dice. If the roll is greater than that model's Wounds characteristic, that model is slain. If the roll is a 6 but is not greater than that model's Wounds characteristic, that model suffers D6 mortal wounds.

6   **Assault of Stone:** *The caster draws forth a slew of sharp rocks that burst from the ground and cascade towards the startled foe.*

Assault of Stone has a casting value of 8. If successfully cast, pick 1 enemy unit wholly within 24" of the caster and visible to them, and roll a number of dice equal to the casting roll. For each roll that is less than that unit's Save characteristic, that unit suffers 1 mortal wound. Rolls of 1 or 2 always fail to inflict a mortal wound on the target. A Save characteristic of '-' counts as a 6 for the purposes of this rule.

GREAT NATION OF YMETRICA

The Ymetricans, known as the Scions of the Peaks, hail from the most mountainous of all the Hyshian nations. They are famed across the Realm of Light for their stoicism. Unflinching and devoted to Teclis' cause, they are a bulwark of skill that can turn aside an enemy blow before channelling the power of the peaks into a deadly riposte.

The warriors of Ymetrica are given to long periods of introspection. With the realms falling apart around them, they have learnt to turn this tendency to their advantage in the theatre of war. Every battle is preceded by a day of contemplation during which the Ymetricans run through every possible permutation of the clash to come. This means that in battle they fight with an incredible surety of action and economy of motion. They let the enemy expend their strength, turning aside attacks with masterful skill, and then capitalise when their adversary is still off balance. To the unenlightened, each cut and thrust seems lightning fast, but in truth it is the culmination of an hours-long thought experiment that leads to one result alone.

The power of the Ymetricans lies not only in sound logic but also in the blessing of the mountains. Each Ymetrican takes with them the magic of their homeland in the form of pieces of enchanted mineral, ranging from aetherquartz gems to stone jewellery, and through these they channel the enduring might of their mountain nation. They turn killing thrusts into glancing blows and reply with strikes powerful enough to split rock, slowly driving the enemy horde back into disarray until they have forced a total rout.

ABILITIES
Mountain Realm: *Ymetrica's people hail from a mountainous realm and can channel the power of stone.*

The Enduring as Rock battle trait (pg 67) changes the Rend characteristic for an attack that targets an **YMETRICA ALARITH** unit in the mountain stance to '-' if the weapon used for that attack has a Rend characteristic of -1 or -2 instead of only -1.

COMMAND ABILITY
Redoubled Force: *Nothing can halt the steady advance of the Alarith warriors that hail from Ymetrica.*

You can use this command ability at the end of the combat phase. If you do so, pick 1 friendly **YMETRICA ALARITH** unit that has just forced an enemy unit to move using the Tectonic Force battle trait (pg 67) for the first time in that phase and that is wholly within 18" of a friendly **YMETRICA HERO**. You can use the Tectonic Force battle trait for a second time by picking 1 other enemy unit within 1" of that friendly unit.

COMMAND TRAIT
An **YMETRICA** general must have this command trait instead of one listed on pages 66-67.

Almighty Blow: *This general can gather their strength and unleash it in a single devastating attack.*

When this general fights, instead of piling in and attacking, you can say that they will unleash a single almighty blow. If you do so, pick 1 enemy unit within 1" of this general and roll a dice. On a 2+, that enemy unit suffers D3 mortal wounds.

ARTEFACT OF POWER
The first **YMETRICA HERO** to receive an artefact of power must be given the Mountains' Gift.

Mountains' Gift: *This weapon contains fragments of rock gifted to the bearer by all of the mountains in Ymetrica. It bears several geomantic enchantments blended as one.*

Pick 1 of the bearer's melee weapons. Once per phase, you can add 1 to the damage inflicted by 1 attack made with that weapon. In addition, roll a dice each time you allocate a wound or mortal to the bearer. On a 6, that wound or mortal wound is negated. In addition, each time the bearer is affected by a spell or endless spell, you can roll a dice. On a 5+, ignore the effects of that spell on the bearer.

# GREAT NATION OF SYAR

The Syari are artisans beyond compare, lavishing years or even decades on the most superb works of craftsmanship that the Mortal Realms have ever seen. When they go to war, they do so in splendour, bedecked in the finest artefacts and armour. In the hands of a Syari warrior, even a tiny jewelled dagger can cut to the heart.

A false dawn glimmers on the horizon as the Syari military march into view. Their phalanxes are clad in such finery that they gleam and shimmer with every movement, throwing scintillating rainbows and orbs of refracted light in all directions. Each warrior is lit by the generous reserves of aetherquartz they wear upon their helms and robes much as a queen might wear her jewels of state. Though they have learnt humility since the Ocari Dara, the Syar show little restraint on the day of war. Having once sworn never again to unleash the full might of their arcane creations, such is the predicament of the Mortal Realms under the scourge of Chaos that they have been forced to employ the most spectacular weapons to keep the hopes of their aelven kin alive. They have come to learn that their base and jealous enemies would see them broken and cast into the mud no matter the cost; such small-minded foes are driven to distraction by the arrogance they wear as a proud cloak about themselves. Yet their finery is no mere decoration. A hulking brute may career headlong towards a slight and preening Syari princeling, only to be cut down in a flash as his rapier-thin blade turns to a slashing beam of sunlight that takes head from neck, leaving behind only a neat, cauterised stump.

ABILITIES

Gleaming Brightness: *The sheer concentration of aetherquartz that the Syar have gathered and fashioned into their raiment of war flaunts their wealth for all to see.*

Syar units start the battle with 2 aetherquartz reserves instead of 1.

COMMAND ABILITY

Deplete Reserves: *The Syar do not hesitate to use their reserves of aetherquartz when it is opportune to do so.*

You can use this command ability when a friendly **Syar** unit could use an aetherquartz reserve ability, even if any friendly **Syar** units have already done so in that turn. If you do so, pick 1 friendly **Syar** unit that has any aetherquartz reserves and is wholly within 18" of a friendly **Syar Hero**. That unit can use 1 of its aetherquartz reserves to use that aetherquartz reserve ability.

COMMAND TRAIT

A **Syar** general must have this command trait instead of one listed on pages 66-67.

Goading Arrogance: *This general uses an appearance of arrogance and superiority as a feint, goading the enemy into foolhardy attacks.*

At the start of the combat phase, you can pick 1 enemy **Hero** within 6" of this general. That enemy **Hero** can only target this general in that phase. In addition, you can add 1 to hit rolls for attacks that target that enemy **Hero** in that phase.

ARTEFACT OF POWER

The first **Syar Hero** to receive an artefact of power must be given The Perfect Blade.

The Perfect Blade: *This blade, understated in appearance, is one of the most perfect weapons ever made.*

Pick 1 of the bearer's melee weapons. An unmodified hit roll of 3+ for an attack made by that weapon always hits the target, an unmodified wound roll of 3+ for an attack made by that weapon is always successful, and an unmodified save roll of 3 or less for an attack made by that weapon always fails.

GREAT NATION OF ILIATHA

The shining hosts of Iliatha are famously close-knit – disturbingly so, in fact, for they house clone-twins that are essentially one mind in two bodies. Even in the mayhem of battle, one regiment will instinctively know which course of action another will take, lending them an uncanny unity and resolve on the battlefield.

It is an open secret that after the depredations of Slaanesh brought the aelven race to the brink of utter extinction, the oft-cursed survivors have been slow to propagate. Not so for Iliatha, where natural childbirth has been augmented – and at times replaced – by the magical process of arcanogenesis. The matriarchs of Iliatha, known as the Mothers of the Spirit, have ensured their people are cloned – not with irresponsible abandon, as in the times leading to the Spirefall, but slowly and carefully. Where two such clone-twins fight alongside one another, they act as one mind in two bodies, and they are all the more lethal for it. Some families ensure that each clone-twin is seconded to a different unit in the Iliathan military, so that they will fight to the last in each other's defence. After all, an Iliathan would no more abandon their clone-twin than they would take their own life. The incredible skill with which the Iliathans manipulate life force is embodied in the artefacts known as simulacra amulets. Upon the bearer's death, a fully fledged and healthy clone will manifest to replace them, as if a mirror image has come to life. This happens much to the killer's surprise, especially given that the new clone's first act is to slay that which killed their former incarnation.

ABILITIES

Soul-bond: *Vanari and aelementiri units from Iliatha are made up of soul-bonded twins, none of whom will desert their siblings either in life or in death.*

Add 2 to the Bravery characteristic of **Iliatha Vanari** and **Iliatha Aelementiri** units.

Unity of Purpose: *The Warden and Sentinel regiments of Iliatha act in unison at a single command.*

After a friendly **Iliatha Vanari** unit uses a command ability, you can pick 1 other friendly **Iliatha Vanari** unit within 3" of that unit. If you do so, that other unit can also use that command ability without spending any command points. You can only use this ability once per phase.

COMMAND ABILITY

Strike in Unison: *This army is made up of soul-bonded twins who act in unison as if one mind were in two bodies.*

You can use this command ability in your shooting phase or in the combat phase. If you do so, pick 1 friendly **Iliatha Vanari** unit with 2 or more models. You can re-roll hit rolls of 1 for that unit.

ARTEFACT OF POWER

The first **Iliatha Hero** to receive an artefact of power must be given the Simulacra Amulet.

Simulacra Amulet: *This finely crafted but innocuous-looking ornament is bonded to the wearer and can swiftly create a healthy clone of the bearer's body in the instant of their death.*

The first time the bearer is slain, before removing them from the battlefield, roll a dice. On a 1-3, the bearer is slain. On a 4-6, the bearer is not slain, all wounds allocated to them are healed and any wounds that currently remain to be allocated to them are negated.

GREAT NATION OF ZAITREC

In a race known for its mastery of the arcane arts, the lambent mystics of Zaitrec are a cut above the rest. Even their youngest Vanari have copious magical talent. The mages of this Great Nation summon the energies of killing light in such abundance that they can melt most of an enemy force into slurry even before the battlelines close.

There was a time when the Lumineth of Zaitrec were content to dwell in the magical light of Hysh's moons, basking in the radiance of Celennar and wondering at the nature of the cosmos. That luxury is long gone. Now, with the Mortal Realms on the brink of dissolution, they turn their innate talents in the eldritch arts to the cause of war. Zaitrec's mages are pre-eminent; taught not only by Teclis but also Celennar, they are able to summon and bind Hyshian energy in hundreds of different ways in order to bend reality to their desires. Something of their wondering, wide-eyed nature remains, however – the Zaitreci find all kinds of magic to be fascinating, whether it is a spell from a dusty tome or the savage chanting of a tribal shaman. They learn at an incredible rate, especially in relation to matters arcane. A rival mage who weaves the same spell twice may find that, though its first incarnation hits home as intended, its second casting is refuted with effortless ease, the Lumineth mage having studied its effects and added it to their lengthy roster of riddles solved and mastered. The most talented of the Zaitreci mages enjoy the direct favour of Celennar; some even bear a gift that protects them, acting as a conduit between the favoured acolyte and the moon spirit.

ABILITIES

Lambent Mystics: *The Lumineth of Zaitrec are exceptionally gifted in the arcane arts. It is said that the power of magic runs through their veins.*

Add 1 to the first casting, dispelling or unbinding roll you make for each friendly **Zaitrec Wizard** in each hero phase. In addition, each **Zaitrec Wizard Hero** knows 1 extra spell from the appropriate spell lore (pg 68-69).

COMMAND TRAIT

A **Zaitrec Wizard** general must have this command trait instead of one listed on pages 66-67.

Fast Learner: *This wizard general is endlessly fascinated by any form of magic, studying it intently in order to unravel its secrets.*

This general can attempt to unbind 1 extra spell in the enemy hero phase. In addition, the second time that this general attempts to unbind a spell in the same enemy hero phase, you can re-roll the unbinding roll.

ARTEFACT OF POWER

The first **Zaitrec Hero** to receive an artefact of power must be given the Gift of Celennar.

Gift of Celennar: *This moonstone talisman protects the bearer from harm. Its power is redoubled in the presence of Celennar.*

Roll a dice each time you allocate a wound or mortal wound to the bearer. Add 2 to the roll if **Teclis** is part of your army and on the battlefield. On a 6+, that wound or mortal wound is negated.

LORE OF ZAITREC

Zaitrec Wizards know the following spell in addition to any other spells that they know.

Overwhelming Heat: *The caster causes the air to grow thicker and thicker with oppressive, overwhelming heat.*

Overwhelming Heat has a casting value of 7. If successfully cast, pick 1 enemy unit wholly within 24" of the caster and visible to them. Halve the Move characteristic of that unit until your next hero phase. Then, roll a dice. If the roll is equal to or greater than that unit's Save characteristic, that unit suffers D3 mortal wounds.

BATTLEPLAN
THE VANGUARD STRIKES

Until recently, the Lumineth Realm-lords have been a reclusive race, rarely venturing beyond the boundaries of their Great Nations in the Realm of Light. Archmage Teclis is determined for this to change, as he fears that without the active participation of the Lumineth in the fight against Chaos, all of the Mortal Realms may be doomed.

To this end, he has started leading powerful vanguards of his kin through Realmgates into the other realms. All those who are foolish enough to oppose the Lumineth are swiftly crushed, like the misguided upstarts that they are.

THE ARMIES
Each player picks an army as described in the core rules. One player is the Lumineth Realm-lords player. Their opponent is the Upstart. The Lumineth Realm-lords player must use a Lumineth Realm-lords army that includes TECLIS.

THE BATTLEFIELD
Set up 1 Baleful Realmgate terrain feature in the centre of the battlefield. Then, set up any further terrain as described in the core rules.

SET-UP
The Lumineth Realm-lords player sets up 3 units from their army wholly within their territory, as shown on the map. TECLIS must not be one of these units. The remaining units in the Lumineth Realm-lords army start the battle in reserve and will arrive as described later (see Command Ability).

The Upstart then picks 1 point on the battlefield edge and sets up 3 units from their army wholly within 9" of that point. The remaining units in the Upstart's army start the battle in reserve and will arrive as described later (see Wrath Awakened).

FIRST TURN
The Lumineth Realm-lords player takes the first turn in the first battle round.

WRATH AWAKENED
As the sound of battle grows, more and more units from the Upstart's army begin to arrive.

At the end of their movement phase, the Upstart can roll a number of dice equal to the number of the current battle round. For each 4+, they can set up 1 reserve unit from their army wholly within 6" of the battlefield edge and more than 9" from any enemy units.

COMMAND ABILITY
The following additional command ability can be used in this battle.

Call for Reinforcements: *The Lumineth can call for reinforcements to help them defend the bridgehead.*

The Lumineth Realm-lords player can use this command ability at the end of their turn if any units from their army are in reserve and if a friendly HERO is on the battlefield and wholly within their own territory. If they do so, they can roll a dice. On a 2+, they can set up 1 reserve unit from their army wholly within 6" of the Baleful Realmgate in the centre of the battlefield and more than 3" from any enemy units.

DESTROY THE REALMGATE
The Upstart quickly realises that the only way to halt this incursion is to destroy the Realmgate.

Units in the Upstart's army treat the Baleful Realmgate in the centre of the battlefield as an enemy model

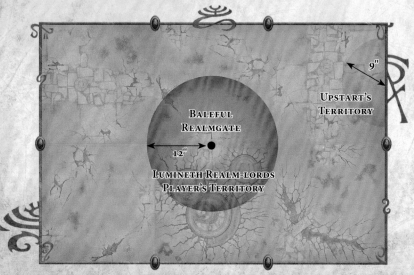

and can attack it with melee weapons (it is not affected by spells or abilities except for those that affect terrain features). That Baleful Realmgate is considered to have a Wounds characteristic of 12 and a Save characteristic of 3+.

BATTLE LENGTH

The battle lasts until the Baleful Realmgate in the centre of the battlefield is destroyed or for 5 battle rounds, whichever happens first.

GLORIOUS VICTORY

If the Baleful Realmgate in the centre of the battlefield is destroyed, the Upstart wins a **major victory**.

If the Baleful Realmgate in the centre of the battlefield has fewer than 6 wounds allocated to it at the end of the battle, the Lumineth Realm-lords player wins a **major victory**.

If neither player has won a **major victory**, the Upstart rolls a dice and adds the number of wounds allocated to the Baleful Realmgate to the roll. If the total is greater than 12, the Upstart wins a **minor victory**. If the total is less than 12, the Lumineth Realm-lords player wins a **minor victory**. If the total is exactly 12, the battle is a **draw**.

SITE OF ENLIGHTENMENT

Standing sentinel over the mountain temples that form the focal points of their bond with their aelementor are the Alarith warriors known as the Stoneguard. Should travellers approach one of these sacred sites, these hitherto serene aelves will move quickly and purposefully to impede their passage, demanding they state their intentions. Any aggressive action on the part of the travellers will be met with intractable defiance by the Stoneguard, who will swiftly be joined in defence of the temple by more of their kin.

THE ARMIES
Each player picks an army as described in the core rules. One player is the Lumineth Realm-lords player and their opponent is the Traveller.

The Lumineth Realm-lords player must use a Lumineth Realm-lords army consisting of 5 units from the following list:

• 1 Alarith Stonemage.

• 0-1 Alarith Spirit of the Mountain.

• 2-4 Alarith Stoneguard units, each of up to 5 models.

• 0-1 Vanari Dawnriders unit of up to 5 models,
   or 0-1 Vanari Auralan Sentinels unit of up to 10 models,
   or 0-1 Vanari Auralan Wardens unit of up to 10 models.

The Traveller's army has 5 units, each of which must conform to a unit type from the following list:

• **Horde unit:** A unit of up to 20 models, each with a Wounds characteristic of 1 and a Save characteristic of 6+ or '-'.

• **Regular unit:** A unit of up to 10 models, each with a Wounds characteristic of 1 and a Save characteristic of 3+, 4+ or 5+.

• **Elite unit:** A unit of up to 5 models, each with a Wounds characteristic of 2 or 3.

• **Guard unit:** A unit of up to 3 models, each with a Wounds characteristic of 4 or 5.

• **Linebreaker unit:** A unit of 1 model with a Wounds characteristic of 6 to 9 that is not a **Hero**.

• **Champion:** A **Hero** that is not a **Monster**.

THE BATTLEFIELD
The Lumineth Realm-lords player must set up 1 terrain feature as shown on the map. That terrain feature is referred to as the Temple in the rules that follow. Set up any further terrain as described in the core rules.

SET-UP
The players alternate setting up units one at a time, starting with the Lumineth Realm-lords player. Players must set up units wholly within their own territory, more than 12" from enemy territory. The territories are shown on the map.

Any Alarith Spirit of the Mountain, Vanari Dawnriders, Vanari Auralan Sentinels or Vanari Auralan Wardens units in the Lumineth Realm-lords player's army start the battle in reserve and will arrive as described opposite.

Continue to set up units until both players have set up their armies. If one player finishes first, their opponent must set up the rest of the units in their army, one after another.

FIRST TURN

The Traveller takes the first turn in the first battle round.

HELP AT HAND

When one Lumineth force is beset, another is usually close at hand.

At the end of their movement phase, the Lumineth Realm-lords player can set up 1 or more reserve units wholly within 6" of the battlefield edge and more than 9" from any enemy units. At the start of the fourth battle round, any models that are still in reserve are slain.

NO QUARTER

The Lumineth will not forsake this site; neither will the enemy retreat.

Do not take battleshock tests for units while they are wholly within 18" of the Temple.

BATTLE LENGTH

The battle lasts for 5 battle rounds.

GLORIOUS VICTORY

At the end of the battle, the player with the most models within 3" of the Temple controls it. If there are no models within 3" of the Temple or the number of models is tied, the Lumineth Realm-lords player controls it.

The player controlling the Temple wins a **major victory** if there are no enemy models within 9" of the Temple and a **minor victory** if there are 1 or more enemy models within 9" of the Temple.

PATH TO GLORY

Path to Glory campaigns centre around collecting and fighting a series of battles in the Mortal Realms. Players start off with a small warband. Over the course of several battles, each warband will gather more followers to join them in their quest for glory and renown.

In order to take part in a Path to Glory campaign, you will need two or more players. Each player will need a **Hero** to be their champion and must then create a warband to follow their champion into battle.

The players fight battles against each other using the warbands they have created. The results of these battles will gain their warbands glory. After battle, warbands may swell in numbers as more warriors flock to their banner, or existing troops may become more powerful.

After gaining sufficient glory or growing your warband enough to dominate all others through sheer weight of numbers, you will be granted a final test. Succeed, and you will be crowned the victor of the campaign, your glory affirmed for all time.

CREATING A WARBAND

In a Path to Glory game, you do not select your army in the normal manner. Instead, you create a warband that consists of a mighty champion, battling to earn the favour of the gods, and their followers. The details and progress of each warband need to be recorded on a warband roster, which you can download for free from games-workshop.com.

To create a warband, simply follow these steps and record the results on your warband roster:

1. First, pick a faction for your warband. Each faction has its own set of warband tables that are used to generate the units in the warband and the rewards they can receive for fighting battles. The warband tables included in this battletome let you collect a Lumineth Realm-lords warband, but other *Warhammer Age of Sigmar* publications include warband tables to let you collect warbands from other factions.

2. Next, choose your warband's champion by selecting one of the options from your faction's champion table. Give your champion a suitably grand name and write this down on your warband roster.

3. Having picked your champion, the next step is to make follower rolls to generate your starting followers. The champion you chose in step 2 will determine how many follower rolls you have. To make a follower roll, pick a column from one of the followers tables and then roll a dice. If you prefer, instead of rolling a dice, you can pick the result from the followers table (this still uses up the roll).

   Sometimes a table will require you to expend two or more rolls, or one roll and a number of Glory Points (see Gaining Glory), in order to use it. Note that the option to expend Glory Points can only be used when you add new followers to your army after a battle (see Rewards of Battle). In either case, in order to generate a follower unit from the table, you must have enough rolls and/ or Glory Points to meet the requirements, and you can then either roll once on the table or pick one result from the table of your choice. If you expend Glory Points, you must reduce your Glory Points total by the amount shown on the table.

   Followers are organised into units. The followers table tells you how many models the unit has. Follower units cannot include additional models, but they can otherwise take any options allowed by their warscroll. Record all of the information about your followers on your warband roster.

4. You can use 1 follower roll to allow your champion to start the campaign with a Champion's

   Reward or to allow 1 of your follower units to start the campaign with a Follower's Reward (see Rewards of Battle).

5. Finally, give your warband a name, one that will inspire respect and dread in your rivals. Your warband is now complete and you can fight your first battle. Good luck!

TO WAR!

Having created a warband, you can now fight battles with it against other warbands taking part in the campaign. You can fight battles as and when you wish, and you can use any of the battleplans available for Warhammer Age of Sigmar. The units you use for a game must be those on your roster.

When you use a Lumineth Realm-lords warband in a Path to Glory game, you can use any of the battle traits from pages 65-67 except for the Lumineth Great Nations battle trait. You cannot use any other Lumineth Realm-lords allegiance abilities.

Any casualties suffered by a warband are assumed to have been replaced in time for its next battle. If your champion is slain in a battle, it is assumed that they were merely injured; they are back to full strength for your next game, thirsty for vengeance!

GAINING GLORY

All of the players in the campaign are vying for glory. The amount of glory they have received is represented by the Glory Points that the warband has accumulated. As a warband's glory increases, it will also attract additional followers, and a warband's champion may be granted rewards.

Warbands receive Glory Points after a battle is complete. If the warband drew or lost the battle, it receives 1

Glory Point. If it won the battle, it receives D3 Glory Points (re-roll a result of 1 if it won a **major victory**).

Add the Glory Points you scored to the total recorded on your roster. Once you have won 10 Glory Points, you will have a chance to win the campaign (see Eternal Glory).

REWARDS OF BATTLE

After each battle, you can take one of the three following options. Alternatively, roll a D3 to determine which option to take.

D3	Option
1	**Additional Followers:** *More loyal followers flock to your banner.*

You receive 1 follower roll that can be used to select a new unit from a followers table and add it to your warband roster. See step 3 of Creating a Warband for details of how to use the followers table to add a unit to your army. Once 5 new units have joined your warband, you will have a chance to win the campaign (see Eternal Glory).

2	**Champion's Reward:** *Your champion's prowess grows.*

Roll on your champion rewards table for your warband and note the result on your warband roster. Your champion can only receive 1 Champion's Reward – if they already have a Champion's Reward, you must take a Follower's Reward instead.

3	**Follower's Reward:** *Your warriors become renowned for mighty deeds.*

Pick 1 unit of followers and then roll on the followers rewards table for your warband. Note the result on your warband roster. A unit can only receive 1 Follower's Reward. If all of your follower units have a Follower's Reward, you must take Additional Followers instead.

ETERNAL GLORY

There are two ways to win a Path to Glory campaign: by Blood or by Might. To win by Blood, your warband must first have 10 Glory Points. To win by Might, your warband must have at least 5 additional units of followers. In either case, you must then fight and win one more battle to win the campaign. If the next battle you fight is tied or lost, you do not receive any Glory Points – just keep on fighting battles until you win the campaign… or another player wins first!

You can shorten or lengthen a campaign by lowering or raising the number of Glory Points needed to win by Blood or the number of extra units that must join a warband to win by Might. For example, for a shorter campaign, you could say that a warband only needs 5 Glory Points before the final fight, or for a longer one, you could say that 15 are needed.

LUMINETH WARBAND TABLES

Use the following tables to determine the champion that leads your warband, the followers that make up the units that fight at their side, and the rewards they receive after battle.

CHAMPION TABLE

Champion	Follower Rolls
Alarith Stonemage	4 units
Scinari Cathallar	4 units

LUMINETH AVATAR FOLLOWERS TABLE
(uses 4 rolls, or 1 roll and 3 Glory Points)

D6	Followers
1-6	Alarith Spirit of the Mountain

RETINUE FOLLOWERS TABLE

D6	Followers
1-2	10 Vanari Auralan Wardens
3-4	5 Vanari Auralan Sentinels
5	5 Vanari Dawnriders
6	5 Alarith Stoneguard

HERO FOLLOWERS TABLE

D6	Followers
1-3	Alarith Stonemage
4-6	Scinari Cathallar

RETINUE FOLLOWERS REWARDS TABLE

D6 Reward

1 Gleaming Brightness: *The sheer concentration of aetherquartz that these warriors have fashioned into their raiment of war flaunts their wealth for all to see.*

This unit starts the battle with 2 aetherquartz reserves instead of 1.

2 Lambent Mystics: *These followers are exceptionally gifted in the arcane arts. It is said that the power of magic runs through their veins.*

Add 1 to the first casting, dispelling or unbinding roll you make for this unit in each hero phase.

3 Soul-bond: *These followers are soul-bonded twins, none of whom will desert their siblings either in life or in death.*

Add 2 to the Bravery characteristic of this unit.

4 Shield of Light: *When these warriors stand together, they radiate a dazzling light that protects them from their foes.*

You can re-roll save rolls of 1 for attacks that target this unit while this unit has 5 or more models.

5 Shafts of Light: *These followers radiate blinding shafts of light that befuddle and disorientate, leaving the foe horribly vulnerable to attack.*

You can re-roll hit rolls of 1 for attacks made with melee weapons by this unit while this unit has 5 or more models.

6 Blessing of Teclis: *Teclis has blessed this unit with a shield of magical energy for its protection.*

Roll a dice each time you allocate a wound or mortal wound to this unit. On a 6, that wound or mortal wound is negated.

CHAMPION AND HERO FOLLOWERS REWARDS TABLE

(Lumineth Avatar followers cannot receive rewards)

2D6 Reward

2 Twin Commanders: *This champion has a soul-bonded twin. They act in unison as if one mind were in two bodies.*

Pick 1 other friendly model in your warband to be this model's twin. In your hero phase, if both of these models are on the battlefield, you receive 1 extra command point.

3 Goading Arrogance: *This champion uses an appearance of arrogance and superiority as a feint, goading the enemy into foolhardy attacks.*

At the start of the combat phase, you can pick 1 enemy **Hero** within 3" of this model. That enemy **Hero** can only target this model in that phase. In addition, you can add 1 to hit rolls for attacks that target that enemy **Hero** in that phase.

4 Swordmaster: *This champion has studied the art of the blade for centuries.*

You can re-roll hit rolls for attacks made with melee weapons by this model.

5 Enduring: *This champion's stamina is legendary.*

Add 2 to this model's Wounds characteristic.

6 Warmaster: *This champion has mastered advanced strategies and tactics of battle.*

If this model is part of your army and on the battlefield at the start of your hero phase, roll a dice. On a 4+, you receive 1 extra command point.

7 Majestic: *Few can look upon this champion and not be awed by their luminous majesty.*

Add 1 to the Bravery characteristic of friendly **Lumineth Realm-lords** units while they are wholly within 12" of this model. In addition, subtract 1 from the Bravery characteristic of enemy units they are within 18" of this model.

8 Loremaster: *Few can rival this champion's knowledge of aelven magic.*

This model knows 1 spell from the Lore of Hysh (pg 68).

9 Mystic: *This champion is exceptionally gifted in the arcane arts. It is said that the power of magic runs through their veins.*

Add 1 to casting, dispelling and unbinding rolls for this model.

10 Mighty: *The blows made by this champion land with shattering might.*

Add 1 to wound rolls for attacks made with melee weapons by this model.

11 Thirst for Knowledge: *This champion is endlessly fascinated by any form of magic, studying it intently in order to unravel its secrets.*

Add 1 to unbinding rolls for this model if the spell they are attempting to unbind has been successfully cast and not unbound at least once before in the battle. Add 2 to unbinding rolls for this model instead of 1 if the spell they are attempting to unbind has been successfully cast and not unbound at least 3 times before in the battle.

12 Artefact of Power: *An ancient artefact of power has come into this champion's possession.*

Randomly generate 1 artefact of power for this model from the appropriate Artefacts of Power table (pg 66-67).

WARSCROLLS

This section includes Lumineth Realm-lords warscrolls, warscroll battalions and endless spell warscrolls. Updated April 2020; the warscrolls printed here take precedence over any warscrolls with an earlier publication date or no publication date.

WARSCROLL BATTALION
TECLIAN VANGUARD

The Teclian Vanguard is a force that has already earned a terrifying reputation as it sallies forth from Hysh into the wider realms. What it lacks in numbers, this strike force more than makes up for in skill, precision and arcane might. The Auralan Legions form its main body, the swift-moving Dawnrider Lances its blade and the Alarith Temple its stony heart. With Teclis' might augmenting all under his aegis, there is nothing it cannot achieve.

ORGANISATION

- Archmage Teclis and Celennar, Spirit of Hysh

- 0-1 The Light of Eltharion

- 1 Alarith Temple battalion

- 1-3 Auralan Legion battalions

- 2 Dawnrider Lance battalions

ABILITIES

Blessing of Teclis: *When a Teclian Vanguard deploys for battle, Teclis creates a shield of magical energy to protect it.*

Roll a dice each time you allocate a wound or mortal wound to a friendly unit from this battalion while it is wholly within its own territory. On a 6, that wound or mortal wound is negated.

WARSCROLL BATTALION
ALARITH TEMPLE

ORGANISATION

- Avalenor, the Stoneheart King or 1 Alarith Spirit of the Mountain

- 1 Alarith Stonemage

- 1-3 units of Alarith Stoneguard

ABILITIES

Skin to Stone: *The Stoneguard of an Alarith Temple can turn aside enemy blows by making their skin become as hard and unyielding as stone.*

At the start of the combat phase, any friendly **Stoneguard** units from this battalion that are wholly within 12" of a friendly **Hero** from the same battalion can turn their skin to stone until the end of that phase. You can re-roll save rolls for attacks that target a unit that has turned its skin to stone, but models in a unit that has turned its skin to stone can only move 1" when they pile in.

WARSCROLL BATTALION
AURALAN LEGION

ORGANISATION

- 1 Scinari Cathallar

- 2-4 units of Vanari Auralan Sentinels and an equal number of units of Vanari Auralan Wardens

ABILITIES

Shield of Light: *When the warriors in an Auralan Legion stand together, they radiate a dazzling light that protects them from their foes.*

You can re-roll save rolls of 1 for attacks that target a friendly unit from this battalion while it is within 3" of any other friendly units from the same battalion.

WARSCROLL BATTALION
DAWNRIDER LANCE

ORGANISATION

- 2-3 units of Vanari Dawnriders

ABILITIES

Shafts of Light: *When a Dawnrider Lance closes with the enemy, it radiates blinding shafts of light that befuddle and disorientate, leaving the foe horribly vulnerable to attack.*

You can re-roll hit rolls of 1 for attacks made with melee weapons by a friendly unit from this battalion that has made a charge move in the same turn.

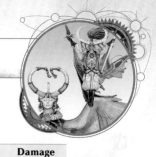

ARCHMAGE TECLIS
AND CELENNAR, SPIRIT OF HYSH

84

16 MOVE

4+ SAVE

10 BRAVERY

WOUNDS

Teclis is a paragon of magical talent, a deific presence who has only become more powerful since uniting his soul with the lunasphinx Celennar. Their mastery of light protects the Lumineth armies whilst searing the foe to scattering ashes.

MISSILE WEAPONS	Range	Attacks	To Hit	To Wound	Rend	Damage
Lunar Staff	18"	1	2+	2+	-3	D6
MELEE WEAPONS	**Range**	**Attacks**	**To Hit**	**To Wound**	**Rend**	**Damage**
Sword of Teclis	1"	2	4+	2+	-3	D3
Moonbright Talons	1"	✸	3+	3+	-2	2

DAMAGE TABLE			
Wounds Suffered	Move	Moonbright Talons	Aura of Celennar
0-4	12"	6	16"
5-7	10"	5	12"
8-10	8"	4	8"
11-13	6"	3	6"
14+	4"	2	4"

DESCRIPTION

Archmage Teclis is a named character that is a single model. He is armed with the Sword of Teclis and the Lunar Staff, and he carries the Discs of the Aelementiri.

CELENNAR: Teclis is accompanied by Celennar, Spirit of Hysh, who attacks with Moonbright Talons. For rules purposes, Celennar is treated in the same manner as a mount.

FLY: This model can fly.

ABILITIES

Archmage: *When Teclis concentrates deeply enough, not even the most powerful wizards in the Mortal Realms can unbind his spells.*

At the start of your hero phase, you must say if this model will cast 1 spell, 2 spells or up to 4 spells. If this model will cast 1 spell, when it attempts to cast that spell, it is automatically cast (do not roll 2D6) and it cannot be unbound.

If this model will cast 2 spells, when it attempts to cast those spells, each is automatically cast with a casting roll of 12 that cannot be modified (do not roll 2D6). Enemy **WIZARDS** can attempt to unbind these spells.

If this model will cast up to 4 spells, when it attempts to cast those spells, each is automatically cast with a casting roll of 10 that cannot be modified (do not roll 2D6). Enemy **WIZARDS** can attempt to unbind these spells.

Aura of Celennar: *The presence of Celennar grants nearby allies arcane knowledge and insight.*

Add 1 to casting, dispelling and unbinding rolls for friendly **LUMINETH REALM-LORDS** units within range of this model's Aura of Celennar ability. The range of the Aura of Celennar ability for this model is shown on the damage table above.

Discs of the Aelementiri: *Teclis has mastered all four aelementiri disciplines. He carries at his belt magical discs that can cause the realm around him to absorb hostile magic.*

In your hero phase, in addition to casting 1, 2 or up to 4 spells, this model can automatically dispel 1 endless spell (do not roll 2D6). In the enemy hero phase, this model can automatically unbind 1 enemy spell (do not roll 2D6).

Seeing Stone of Celennar: *A priceless gift from Celennar to Teclis, this allows the bearer to see the flow of magic itself – and alter it to his whim.*

Each time a friendly unit within range of this model's Aura of Celennar ability is affected by an endless spell or a spell cast by an enemy **WIZARD**, you can roll a dice. On a 4+, ignore the effects of that spell or endless spell on that unit. Then, pick 1 enemy unit within 18" of that unit. That enemy unit suffers D3 mortal wounds. The range of the Aura of Celennar ability for this model is shown on the damage table above.

MAGIC

Teclis is a **WIZARD**. The number of spells that he can cast is determined using the Archmage ability on the left. He can attempt to unbind any number of spells in the enemy hero phase. He knows the Arcane Bolt, Mystic Shield, Protection of Teclis and Storm of Searing White Light spells.

Protection of Teclis: *Teclis opens his arms wide, creating a field of glowing energy that protects all of his allies that are nearby.*

Protection of Teclis has a casting value of 10. If successfully cast, until your next hero phase, roll a dice each time you allocate a wound or mortal wound to a friendly unit wholly within 18" of the caster. On a 5+, that wound or mortal wound is negated. This spell cannot be cast in the same hero phase as Protection of Hysh.

Storm of Searing White Light: *Beams of light shoot out from the caster's forehead, cleaving through nearby enemies.*

Storm of Searing White Light has a casting value of 10. If successfully cast, roll a dice for each enemy unit within 18" of the caster and visible to them. On a 1, nothing happens. On a 2-4, that unit suffers D3 mortal wounds. On a 5+, that unit suffers D6 mortal wounds.

KEYWORDS	ORDER, AELF, LUMINETH REALM-LORDS, MONSTER, HERO, WIZARD, TECLIS

THE LIGHT OF ELTHARION

		MOVE 6"		
WOUNDS 7		✕	SAVE 3+	
		10		
		BRAVERY		

Eltharion has no physical form, only a spiritual essence given uncanny strength through Teclis' magic. An ancestor of the Lumineth race, his avenging spirit is a puissant warrior and an inspiring hero to those aelves who witness his shining light.

MELEE WEAPONS	Range	Attacks	To Hit	To Wound	Rend	Damage
Fangsword of Eltharion	1"	4	2+	3+	-3	D3
Celennari Blade	1"	2	2+	3+	-1	D3

DESCRIPTION

The Light of Eltharion is a named character that is a single model. He is armed with the Fangsword of Eltharion and the Celennari Blade, and he wears Spirit Armour.

ABILITIES

Celennari Blade: *This blade was forged by Teclis using Celennar's scryer-stone ores. The lunar gem in its hilt allows the bearer to predict where an opponent will be most vulnerable.*

At the start of the combat phase, you can pick 1 enemy **Hero** within 3" of this model. If you do so, add 1 to the damage inflicted by successful attacks made with this model's Celennari Blade that target that **Hero** in that phase.

Fangsword of Eltharion: *The original Fangsword was a powerful heirloom of Eltharion's mortal dynasty. The incarnation of the Fangsword wielded by the Light of Eltharion is crafted from sunmetal and has a solar jewel in its hilt, making it even mightier than the sword whose legacy it propagates.*

Add 1 to wound rolls for attacks made with this model's Fangsword of Eltharion if this model made a charge move in the same turn. In addition, if the unmodified wound roll for an attack made with this model's Fangsword of Eltharion is 6, that attack inflicts 1 mortal wound on the target in addition to any normal damage.

Searing Darts of Light: *Darts of brilliance hurtle from the Light of Eltharion's outstretched fingers, shooting through nearby enemies.*

In your shooting phase, you can pick 1 enemy unit within 18" of this model that is visible to them and roll a dice. On a 1, nothing happens. On a 2-4, that unit suffers D3 mortal wounds. On a 5+, that unit suffers D6 mortal wounds.

Spirit Armour: *Instead of protecting a body of flesh and blood, this armour houses the undying spirit of the mighty warrior Eltharion. Though animated by the Light of Eltharion, it is essentially hollow – even a penetrating thrust may simply pass through the glowing form within.*

Ignore modifiers (positive or negative) when making save rolls for attacks that target this model. In addition, halve the damage inflicted by attacks made with missile weapons or melee weapons that target this model (rounding up).

Supreme Swordmaster: *The Light of Eltharion is a consummate warrior and one of the greatest swordsmen of all time.*

Ignore negative modifiers when making hit rolls for attacks made by this model. In addition, if the unmodified hit roll for an attack made by this model is 6, that attack scores 2 hits on the target instead of 1. Make a wound and save roll for each hit.

COMMAND ABILITY

Unflinching Valour: *The Light of Eltharion can communicate telepathically with the warriors of the Lumineth Realm-lords, instilling them with his own dour certainty and unwavering courage.*

You can use this command ability at the start of the battleshock phase. If you do so, pick 1 friendly model with this command ability. Until the end of that phase, all friendly **Lumineth Realm-lords** units wholly within 24" of that model are treated as having a Bravery characteristic of 10.

KEYWORDS	ORDER, AELF, LUMINETH REALM-LORDS, HERO, LIGHT OF ELTHARION

MOVE	6"
WOUNDS	5
SAVE	5+
BRAVERY	7

SCINARI CATHALLAR

The Scinari Cathallar is the single point of darkness in the shining host of their fellow Lumineth. They take the emotional trauma from their kin and weaponise it, unleashing this torment at the foe to render them crippled by angst and despair.

MELEE WEAPONS	Range	Attacks	To Hit	To Wound	Rend	Damage
Despairing Touch	1"	1	4+	2+	-	D3

DESCRIPTION

A Scinari Cathallar is a single model armed with a Despairing Touch.

ABILITIES

Emotional Transference: *A Scinari Cathallar is capable of drawing forth any feelings of despair or doom from nearby Lumineth and redirecting these emotions to afflict the foe.*

At the start of the battleshock phase, you can pick 1 friendly **LUMINETH REALM-LORDS** unit wholly within 18" of this model and roll a dice. On a 2+, do not take a battleshock test for that unit. In addition, if any models from that unit were slain during that turn, you can pick 1 enemy unit within 18" of this model that has to take a battleshock test in that phase. If you do so, add the number of models from that friendly unit that were slain during that turn to the modified battleshock roll for that enemy unit.

MAGIC

This model is a **WIZARD**. It can attempt to cast 1 spell in your hero phase and attempt to unbind 1 spell in the enemy hero phase. It knows the Arcane Bolt, Mystic Shield and Darkness of the Soul spells.

Darkness of the Soul: *The caster fills the minds of their enemies with dark thoughts and negative emotions, making it hard for them to do anything other than contemplate their own futile existence.*

Darkness of the Soul has a casting value of 7. If successfully cast, pick 1 enemy unit within 18" of the caster and visible to them. Until your next hero phase, roll 2D6 each time that unit makes a normal move, makes a charge move, shoots or fights. Make the roll before the action is carried out. If the roll is greater than that unit's Bravery characteristic, that unit cannot perform that action in that phase.

KEYWORDS	ORDER, AELF, LUMINETH REALM-LORDS, SCINARI, HERO, WIZARD, CATHALLAR

The shifting crystal walls of Haixiah would drive a lesser race to madness in hours, but with a Scinari Cathallar to assuage their despair, the aelves of Hysh can strike back against their foes even in the most hostile magical environments.

MOVE 14"
WOUNDS 2
SAVE 4+
BRAVERY 7

VANARI DAWNRIDERS

The Dawnriders charge the foe in tight formation, thundering into the enemy ranks and punching their lances through the chests of their foremost adversaries before leaping over their corpses so that their noble steeds might trample those behind.

MELEE WEAPONS	Range	Attacks	To Hit	To Wound	Rend	Damage
Guardian's Sword	1"	2	3+	4+	-1	1
Sunmetal Lance	2"	1	3+	4+	-	1
Dashing Hooves	1"	2	4+	4+	-	1

DESCRIPTION

A unit of Vanari Dawnriders has any number of models, each armed with a Sunmetal Lance.

MOUNT: This unit's stallion steeds attack with their Dashing Hooves.

STEEDMASTER: 1 model in this unit can be a Steedmaster. A Steedmaster is armed with a Sunmetal Lance and a Guardian's Sword.

STANDARD BEARER: 1 in every 5 models in this unit can be a Standard Bearer. You can re-roll battleshock tests for units that include any Standard Bearers.

ABILITIES

Deathly Furrows: *Vanari Dawnriders scythe through enemy infantry, trampling over lesser foes and carving a furrow of death through the enemy ranks.*

At the start of the combat phase, you can say that this unit will use its Deathly Furrows ability. If you do so, in that phase, you can either add 1 to the Attacks characteristic of this unit's melee

weapons, but it can only target units that have a Wounds characteristic of 1 or 2 and do not have a mount, or you can add 2 to the Attacks characteristic of this unit's melee weapons, but it can only target units that have a Wounds characteristic of 1 and do not have a mount.

Lances of the Dawn: *When Vanari Dawnriders charge full pelt at the foe, their lances can punch through the thickest of armour in a blaze of light and explosive magical power.*

If this unit made a charge move in the same turn, add 1 to wound rolls for attacks made with this unit's Sunmetal Lances and improve the Rend characteristic of that weapon by 1.

Sunmetal Weapons: *The lances used by Vanari Dawnriders are tipped with pure sunmetal that can burn a victim from the inside out.*

If the unmodified hit roll for an attack made with a Sunmetal Lance is 6, that attack inflicts 1 mortal wound on the target and the attack sequence ends (do not make a wound or save roll).

MAGIC

The Steedmaster of this unit is a **WIZARD** while this unit has 3 or more models. They can attempt to cast 1 spell in your hero phase and attempt to unbind 1 spell in the enemy hero phase. They know the Power of Hysh spell.

Power of Hysh: *Lumineth wizards can use their arcane arts to empower sunmetal, making it burn with an even greater intensity.*

Power of Hysh has a casting value of 6. If successfully cast, until your next hero phase, the Sunmetal Weapons ability for the caster and/or the unit they are part of causes mortal wounds to be inflicted on an unmodified hit roll of 5+ instead of 6.

Any number of **LUMINETH REALM-LORDS WIZARDS** can attempt to cast Power of Hysh in the same hero phase.

KEYWORDS	ORDER, AELF, LUMINETH REALM-LORDS, VANARI, DAWNRIDERS

88 · MOVE 6" · WOUNDS 1 · SAVE 5+ · BRAVERY 6

VANARI AURALAN SENTINELS

Master archers, the Auralan Sentinels wield complex aelven bows that can either fire straight and true or loft arrows high in the air to curve down onto distant foes. When their High Sentinel channels power into their arrowheads, they are all the more lethal.

MISSILE WEAPONS	Range	Attacks	To Hit	To Wound	Rend	Damage
Auralan Bow: Aimed	18"	1	3+	4+	-1	1
Auralan Bow: Lofted	30"	1	4+	4+	-	1
MELEE WEAPONS	Range	Attacks	To Hit	To Wound	Rend	Damage
Champion's Blade	1"	2	3+	4+	-1	1
Vanari Dagger	1"	1	3+	4+	-	1

DESCRIPTION

A unit of Vanari Auralan Sentinels has any number of models, each armed with an Auralan Bow and Vanari Dagger.

HIGH SENTINEL: 1 model in this unit can be a High Sentinel. A High Sentinel is armed with a Champion's Blade instead of an Auralan Bow and Vanari Dagger, and they carry a Scryhawk Lantern.

ABILITIES

Scryhawk Lantern: *Every High Sentinel carries a lantern upon their back. Sharp-eyed scryhawks are drawn to its gentle light, over time forming a bond with the archers below. By hovering over the foe, these hawks direct their masters' aim towards any enemies that may be hidden from sight.*

At the start of your shooting phase, you can pick 1 enemy unit within 30" of this unit's High Sentinel that is not visible to them. If you do so, you must choose the Lofted missile weapon characteristic for all attacks made with this unit's Auralan Bows in that phase, but that enemy unit is treated as being visible to all friendly models from this unit until the end of that phase.

Many-stringed Weapon: *An Auralan bow is a flexible weapon that can either fire arrows in aimed shots on a flat trajectory or loft them towards a distant target.*

Before attacking with Auralan Bows, choose either the Aimed or Lofted missile weapon characteristics for all shooting attacks made by this unit in that phase.

Sunmetal Weapons: *The arrows used by Auralan Sentinels are tipped with pure sunmetal that can burn a victim from the inside out.*

If the unmodified hit roll for an attack made with an Auralan Bow is 6, that attack inflicts 1 mortal wound on the target and the attack sequence ends (do not make a wound or save roll).

MAGIC

The High Sentinel of this unit is a **WIZARD** while this unit has 5 or more models. They can attempt to cast 1 spell in your hero phase and attempt to unbind 1 spell in the enemy hero phase. They know the Power of Hysh spell.

Power of Hysh: *Lumineth wizards can use their arcane arts to empower sunmetal, making it burn with an even greater intensity.*

Power of Hysh has a casting value of 6. If successfully cast, until your next hero phase, the Sunmetal Weapons ability for the caster and/or the unit they are part of causes mortal wounds to be inflicted on an unmodified hit roll of 5+ instead of 6.

Any number of **LUMINETH REALM-LORDS WIZARDS** can attempt to cast Power of Hysh in the same hero phase.

KEYWORDS	ORDER, AELF, LUMINETH REALM-LORDS, VANARI, AURALAN SENTINELS

VANARI AURALAN WARDENS

MOVE	6"					
WOUNDS	1		SAVE	4+		
	6					
BRAVERY						

The Auralan Wardens fight in close formation, using long pikes that they set to receive the charge of the foe. The Wardens guide their sunmetal tips into the enemy's chests at the last moment; those pierced by them are slain in a heartbeat.

MELEE WEAPONS	Range	Attacks	To Hit	To Wound	Rend	Damage
Champion's Blade	1"	2	3+	4+	-1	1
Warden's Pike	3"	2	3+	4+	-	1

DESCRIPTION

A unit of Vanari Auralan Wardens has any number of models, each armed with a Warden's Pike.

HIGH WARDEN: 1 model in this unit can be a High Warden. A High Warden is armed with a Champion's Blade instead of a Warden's Pike.

ABILITIES

Moonfire Flask: *The High Warden carries a Moonfire Flask in one hand; when the enemy draws close, the Warden hurls the fragile flask into its ranks so that it bursts and scatters burning silvery liquid all around.*

Once per battle, at the start of the combat phase, you can pick 1 enemy unit within 3" of this unit's High Warden and roll a dice. On a 2+, that enemy unit suffers D3 mortal wounds.

Sunmetal Weapons: *The pikes used by Auralan Wardens are tipped with pure sunmetal that can burn a victim from the inside out.*

If the unmodified hit roll for an attack made with a Warden's Pike is 6, that attack inflicts 1 mortal wound on the target and the attack sequence ends (do not make a wound or save roll).

Wall of Blades: *When Auralan Wardens stand shoulder to shoulder, they present a bristling wall of pikes towards the foe.*

If the target unit made a charge move in the same turn, add 1 to wound rolls for attacks made with this unit's Warden's Pikes and improve the Rend characteristic of that weapon by 1.

MAGIC

The High Warden of this unit is a **WIZARD** while this unit has 5 or more models. They can attempt to cast 1 spell in your hero phase and attempt to unbind 1 spell in the enemy hero phase. They know the Power of Hysh spell.

Power of Hysh: *Lumineth wizards can use their arcane arts to empower sunmetal, making it burn with an even greater intensity.*

Power of Hysh has a casting value of 6. If successfully cast, until your next hero phase, the Sunmetal Weapons ability for the caster and/or the unit they are part of causes mortal wounds to be inflicted on an unmodified hit roll of 5+ instead of 6.

Any number of **LUMINETH REALM-LORDS WIZARDS** can attempt to cast Power of Hysh in the same hero phase.

KEYWORDS	ORDER, AELF, LUMINETH REALM-LORDS, VANARI, AURALAN WARDENS

90

MOVE 6"
WOUNDS 5
SAVE 5+
8
BRAVERY

ALARITH STONEMAGE

First amongst Teclis' disciples to learn the ways of the aelementiri, the Stonemages bring the might of the mountain to the battlefield. They can control rocks, boulders and even gravity itself to crush and confound their adversaries.

MELEE WEAPONS	Range	Attacks	To Hit	To Wound	Rend	Damage
Staff of the High Peaks	3"	D3	3+	3+	-1	D3

DESCRIPTION
An Alarith Stonemage is a single model armed with a Staff of the High Peaks.

ABILITIES
Stonemage Stance: *A Stonemage is able to adopt a stance that allows them to deliver blows with shattering force. Nearby Alarith Stoneguard can emulate their movements to land equally powerful attacks.*

At the start of the combat phase, you can say that this model will adopt the Stonemage Stance. If you do so, this model and any friendly **ALARITH STONEGUARD** units wholly within 12" of this model cannot make a pile-in move in that phase. However, until the end of that phase, improve the Rend characteristic of melee weapons used by this model and those friendly units by 1.

MAGIC
This model is a **WIZARD**. It can attempt to cast 1 spell in your hero phase and attempt to unbind 1 spell in the enemy hero phase. It knows the Arcane Bolt, Mystic Shield and Gravitic Redirection spells.

Gravitic Redirection: *The caster reduces gravity around them to almost zero, redirecting the force to weigh down a nearby foe.*

Gravitic Redirection has a casting value of 5. If successfully cast, until your next hero phase, the caster can fly.

In addition, you can pick 1 enemy unit within 18" of the caster. If you do so, that unit suffers 1 mortal wound and, until your next hero phase, that unit's Move characteristic is halved and it cannot fly.

KEYWORDS ORDER, AELF, LUMINETH REALM-LORDS, AELEMENTIRI, ALARITH, HERO, WIZARD, STONEMAGE

MOVE 4"
WOUNDS 2
SAVE 4+
7
BRAVERY

ALARITH STONEGUARD

The Alarith temples accept the mountain as their master and, in doing so, inherit part of its strength and resilience. They fight as immovable objects, wielding magical hammers that can crush enemy skulls in a single, perfectly measured blow.

MELEE WEAPONS	Range	Attacks	To Hit	To Wound	Rend	Damage
Stone Mallet or Diamondpick Hammer	1"	2	3+	3+	-1	1
Stratum Hammer(s)	1"	3	3+	4+	-	1

DESCRIPTION
A unit of Alarith Stoneguard has any number of models. The unit is armed with one of the following weapon options: Stone Mallet; or Diamondpick Hammer.

TRUESTONE SENESCHAL: 1 model in this unit can be a Truestone Seneschal. A Truestone Seneschal can be armed with a pair of Stratum Hammers instead of the unit's weapon option.

STANDARD BEARER: 1 in every 5 models in this unit can be a Standard Bearer. A Standard Bearer is armed with a Stratum Hammer instead of the unit's weapon option. You can re-roll battleshock tests for units that include any Standard Bearers.

ABILITIES
Crushing Blow: *The Stoneguard land blows with the power of a mountain avalanche.*

If the unmodified hit roll for an attack made with a Stone Mallet is 6, add 1 to the damage inflicted if that attack is successful.

Diamondpick Hammer: *The diamond spike on this hammer can pierce through any armour.*

If the unmodified hit roll for an attack made with a Diamondpick Hammer is 6, that attack inflicts 1 mortal wound on the target and the attack sequence ends (do not make a wound or save roll).

Pair of Stratum Hammers: *A stratum hammer carries the weight of aeons-old rock.*

You can re-roll hit rolls for a pair of Stratum Hammers.

KEYWORDS ORDER, AELF, LUMINETH REALM-LORDS, AELEMENTIRI, ALARITH, STONEGUARD

ALARITH SPIRIT OF THE MOUNTAIN

MOVE 6"

WOUNDS 12

SAVE 3+

BRAVERY 10

Spirits of the Mountain are the war forms of the stony peaks that the Alarith temples have taken as their patrons. Avatars of incredible toughness and strength, they can smash castle gates and steam tanks with a single swing of their worldhammers.

MISSILE WEAPONS	Range	Attacks	To Hit	To Wound	Rend	Damage
Geomantic Blast	✸	1	3+	2+	-2	D6
MELEE WEAPONS	Range	Attacks	To Hit	To Wound	Rend	Damage
Stoneheart Worldhammer	3"	4	3+	2+	-2	✸
Cloven Hooves	1"	2	3+	3+	-1	2

DAMAGE TABLE			
Wounds Suffered	Geomantic Blast	Stoneheart Worldhammer	Stoneheart Shockwave
0-2	30"	5	12"
3-5	25"	4	10"
6-7	20"	3	8"
8-10	15"	2	6"
11+	10"	1	4"

DESCRIPTION

An Alarith Spirit of the Mountain is a single model armed with a Geomantic Blast, Stoneheart Worldhammer and Cloven Hooves.

ABILITIES

All but Immovable: *A Spirit of the Mountain is at its most dangerous when it pauses, plants its feet solidly on the ground and takes careful stock of its surroundings before inflicting carnage upon its enemies.*

If this model does not make a charge move in your charge phase, add 1 to the Attacks characteristic of this model's melee weapons until your next movement phase.

Ponderous Advice: *A Lumineth commander can draw upon the ancient wisdom of a Spirit of the Mountain as long as they are willing to wait long enough for its carefully considered advice.*

At the end of your hero phase, you can pick 1 friendly **Lumineth Realm-lords Aelf Hero** within 3" of this model. If that **Lumineth Realm-lords Aelf Hero** is within 3" of this model at the start of your next hero phase, then that **Lumineth Realm-lords Aelf Hero** can use a command ability in that turn without spending any command points.

Stoneheart Shockwave: *When a Spirit of the Mountain smashes its worldhammer into the ground, it can direct the resulting shockwave at a nearby foe, hurling the enemy to its knees.*

At the start of the enemy shooting phase and at the start of any combat phase, you can pick 1 enemy unit within range of this model's Stoneheart Shockwave ability that is visible to this model. The range of the Stoneheart Shockwave ability for this model is shown on the damage table above. If you do so, subtract 1 from hit rolls for that unit until the end of that phase. A unit cannot be affected by this ability more than once per phase.

Stonemage Symbiosis: *Stonemages are able to sustain a Spirit of the Mountain, allowing them to fight to their fullest potential.*

When you look up a value on this model's damage table, if this model is within 12" of a friendly **Stonemage**, this model is treated as if it has suffered 0 wounds.

COMMAND ABILITY

Faith of the Mountains: *A Spirit of the Mountain can inspire its aelven supplicants to fight all the harder in the name of Hysh.*

You can use this command ability at the start of the combat phase. If you do so, pick 1 friendly **Alarith Aelf** unit wholly within 18" of a friendly model with this command ability. Add 1 to the Attacks characteristic of that unit's melee weapons in that combat phase. A unit cannot benefit from this command ability more than once per combat phase, and a unit cannot benefit from this ability and the Unshakeable Faith of the Mountains command ability in the same phase.

KEYWORDS	ORDER, LUMINETH REALM-LORDS, ALARITH, MONSTER, SPIRIT OF THE MOUNTAIN

AVALENOR
THE STONEHEART KING

MOVE		
	6"	
WOUNDS 14	✕	3+ SAVE
	10	
	BRAVERY	

92

Of all the mountain spirits that march alongside the Lumineth, Avalenor is the eldest and the wisest. Unlike his fellows, he came to the aid of the aelves of his own accord and has been wielding his magical hammers in the name of Hysh ever since.

MISSILE WEAPONS	Range	Attacks	To Hit	To Wound	Rend	Damage
Geomantic Blast	☀	1	3+	2+	-2	D6
MELEE WEAPONS	**Range**	**Attacks**	**To Hit**	**To Wound**	**Rend**	**Damage**
Firestealer Hammers	2"	6	3+	3+	-1	☀
Cloven Hooves	1"	2	3+	3+	-1	2

DAMAGE TABLE			
Wounds Suffered	Geomantic Blast	Guardian of Hysh	Firestealer Hammers
0-3	30"	12"	5
4-6	25"	6"	4
7-9	20"	3"	3
10-12	15"	2"	2
13+	10"	1"	1

DESCRIPTION

Avalenor, the Stoneheart King, is a named character that is a single model. He is armed with a Geomantic Blast, the Firestealer Hammers and Cloven Hooves.

ABILITIES

All but Immovable: *A Spirit of the Mountain is at its most dangerous when it pauses, plants its feet solidly on the ground and takes careful stock of its surroundings before inflicting carnage upon its enemies.*

If this model does not make a charge move in your charge phase, add 1 to the Attacks characteristic of this model's melee weapons until your next movement phase.

Firestealer Hammers: *The Firestealer Hammers channel the intense and freezing temperatures of Avalenor's peak.*

If the unmodified hit roll for an attack made with the Firestealer Hammers is 6, that attack inflicts 1 mortal wound on the target in addition to any normal damage.

Elder Wisdom: *Those with the patience to earn the Stoneheart King's trust will find themselves enlightened for the rest of their living days.*

At the end of your hero phase, you can pick 1 friendly **LUMINETH REALM-LORDS AELF HERO** within 6" of this model. If that **LUMINETH REALM-LORDS AELF HERO** is within 6" of this model at the start of your next hero phase, then that **LUMINETH REALM-LORDS AELF HERO** can use a command ability in that turn without spending any command points.

Guardian of Hysh: *It is said that Avalenor is formed entirely of aetherquartz, causing him to glow with a dazzling light in even the darkest of locations.*

Subtract 1 from hit rolls for attacks made by enemy models that are within range of this model's Guardian of Hysh ability. The range of the Guardian of Hysh ability for this model is shown on the damage table above.

Stonemage Symbiosis: *Stonemages are able to sustain a Spirit of the Mountain, allowing them to fight to their fullest potential.*

When you look up a value on this model's damage table, if this model is within 12" of a friendly **STONEMAGE**, this model is treated as if it has suffered 0 wounds.

COMMAND ABILITY

Unshakeable Faith of the Mountains: *Avalenor inspires total confidence in his aelven supplicants.*

You can use this command ability at the start of the combat phase. If you do so, pick up to D3 friendly **ALARITH AELF** units wholly within 24" of a friendly model with this command ability. Add 1 to the Attacks characteristic of those units' melee weapons in that combat phase. A unit cannot benefit from this command ability more than once per combat phase, and a unit cannot benefit from this ability and the Faith of the Mountains command ability in the same phase.

KEYWORDS	ORDER, LUMINETH REALM-LORDS, ALARITH, YMETRICA, MONSTER, HERO, SPIRIT OF THE MOUNTAIN, AVALENOR

The Stoneheart King strides from the golden light of dawn with hammers raised. The legendary aelementor is Ymetrica's immortal sentience in its war form, harder than stone and with the slow-burning anger of the mountains behind each shattering blow.

HYSHIAN TWINSTONES

Pairs of prism-like jewels easily the size of the mages who conjure them, in times of great peril, Hyshian Twinstones can be wrenched from the heart of the Realm of Light to manifest as reservoirs of arcane power. As one is exhausted, the other regenerates its magical force, harnessing the aetheric energy expended around it in a constant feedback loop.

DESCRIPTION

Hyshian Twinstones is a single model.

PREDATORY: Hyshian Twinstones is a predatory endless spell. It can move up to 8" and can fly.

MAGIC

Summon Hyshian Twinstones: *The caster calls forth two giant crystal teardrops that orbit around each other.*

Summon Hyshian Twinstones has a casting value of 7. Only **Lumineth Realm-lords Wizards** can attempt to cast this spell. If successfully cast, set up 1 Hyshian Twinstones model wholly within 6" of the caster.

ABILITIES

Reservoir of Power: *The twinstones glow brighter with each spell cast, forming a reservoir from which the Lumineth can draw greater power.*

When this model is set up, place a D6 beside it with the 1 facing up. Each time a spell is successfully cast by a unit within 12" of this model and not unbound, after the effects of the spell have been resolved, increase the value of the dice beside this model by 1 (to a maximum of 6).

If a **Lumineth Realm-lords Wizard** attempts to cast a spell while they are within 12" of this model, before making the casting roll, the player controlling that **Wizard** can say that they will draw on the power of the twinstones. If they do so, add the value of the dice beside this

model to the casting roll. Then, after the effects of the spell have been resolved, change the value of the dice beside this model back to 1.

KEYWORDS	ENDLESS SPELL, HYSHIAN TWINSTONES

SANCTUM OF AMYNTOK

The ground splits to form a ritual circle around the mage and the life force of the realm springs forth in a crackling shield. Based around the rune Yngra, a sigil synonymous with rescue as well as imprisonment, the shield turns baleful spells and attacks into flashes of blinding light.

DESCRIPTION

The Sanctum of Amyntok is a single endless spell that consists of 3 models (if it is dispelled, remove all 3 models).

MAGIC

Summon Sanctum of Amyntok: *The ground splits around the mage, and the life force of the realm springs forth as a crackling shield.*

Summon Sanctum of Amyntok has a casting value of 7. Only **Lumineth Realm-lords Wizards** can attempt to cast this spell.

If successfully cast, set up 1 Sanctum of Amyntok model wholly within 3" of the caster and more than 3" from any other units. Then, set up the second and third Sanctum of Amyntok models so that the tip of each model is touching the tip

of a different model from the same endless spell, with each model more than 3" from any other units and with the caster inside the ring.

As long as the Sanctum of Amyntok remains on the battlefield, the caster and the Sanctum of Amyntok are treated as being a single model from the caster's army that uses the caster's warscroll as well as the Endless Spells rules. It is treated as an enemy model by the opposing player's army.

If the caster is slain, then the Sanctum of Amyntok is immediately dispelled and removed from play along with the caster. If the Sanctum of Amyntok is dispelled and the caster has not been slain, remove the endless spell models from play and leave the caster on the battlefield.

ABILITIES

Sigil of Yngra: *The sanctum turns baleful spells and attacks into flashes of blinding light.*

Subtract 1 from hit rolls and add 1 to save rolls for attacks that target this model.

In addition, at the end of the combat phase, if this model was targeted by any enemy attacks during that phase, roll a dice for each enemy unit within 3" of this model. On a 1-3, nothing happens. On a 4-5, that enemy unit suffers 1 mortal wound. On a 6, that enemy unit suffers D3 mortal wounds.

KEYWORDS	ENDLESS SPELL, SANCTUM OF AMYNTOK

RUNE OF PETRIFICATION

The dreaded Rune of Petrification is unleashed only in the direst peril, for once it has been summoned, it cannot easily be dispelled – and its curse is fearsome indeed. Those enemies who linger nearby will find their flesh hardening and turning to stone until they are but inert statues, monuments to their own folly in opposing the Lumineth.

DESCRIPTION

The Rune of Petrification is a single model.

MAGIC

Summon Rune of Petrification: *The caster calls forth a hovering sigil ripped from the crust of the realm underfoot.*

Summon Rune of Petrification has a casting value of 8. Only LUMINETH REALM-LORDS WIZARDS can attempt to cast this spell. If successfully cast, set up 1 Rune of Petrification model wholly within 18" of the caster.

ABILITIES

Turn to Stone: *Any foes who remain too close to this hovering sigil will find their flesh hardening and turning into stone, until soon they are nothing more than lifelike statues.*

At the start of the movement phase and at the end of the movement phase, roll a dice for each unit that is within 6" of this model. On a 4+, that unit suffers D3 mortal wounds.

In addition, subtract 1 from run and charge rolls for units within 6" of this model. This ability has no effect on LUMINETH REALM-LORDS units.

KEYWORDS	ENDLESS SPELL, RUNE OF PETRIFICATION

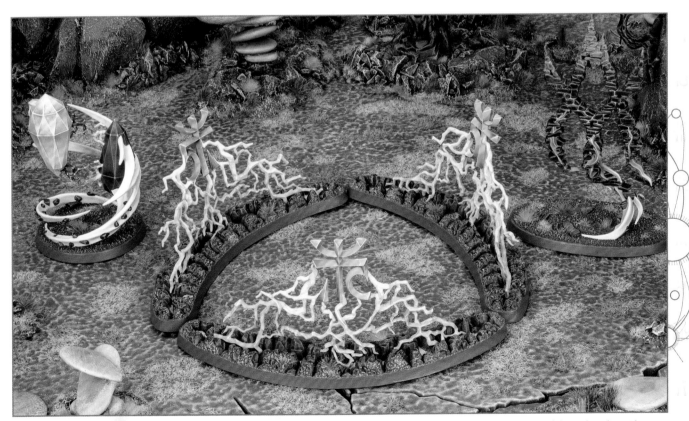

The endless spells cast by the Lumineth are not traditional manifestations of magic. Rather, they are the innate power of the realms themselves, given shape and utilised as sources of energy, potent defences or deadly weapons.

PITCHED BATTLE PROFILES

The table below provides points, minimum and maximum unit sizes and battlefield roles for the warscrolls and warscroll battalions in this book, for use in Pitched Battles. Spending the points listed on this table allows you to take a minimum-sized unit with any of its upgrades. Understrength units cost the full amount of points. Larger units are taken in multiples of their minimum unit size; multiply their cost by the same amount as you multiplied their size. If a unit has two points values separated by a slash (e.g. '60/200'), the second value is for a maximum-sized unit. Units that are listed as 'Unique' are named characters and can only be taken once in an army. A unit that has any of the keywords listed in the Allies table can be taken as an allied unit. Updated April 2020; the profiles printed here take precedence over any profiles with an earlier publication date or no publication date.

LUMINETH REALM-LORDS UNIT	UNIT SIZE MIN	UNIT SIZE MAX	POINTS	BATTLEFIELD ROLE	NOTES
Vanari Auralan Wardens	10	30	120	Battleline	For each Vanari Auralan Wardens unit included in your army, you can take 1 Vanari Auralan Sentinels unit or 1 Vanari Dawnriders unit as a battleline unit
Alarith Spirit of the Mountain	1	1	340	Behemoth	
Alarith Stonemage	1	1	130	Leader	
Scinari Cathallar	1	1	140	Leader	
The Light of Eltharion	1	1	220	Leader	Unique
Archmage Teclis and Celennar, Spirit of Hysh	1	1	660	Leader, Behemoth	Unique
Avalenor, the Stoneheart King	1	1	360	Leader, Behemoth	Unique
Alarith Stoneguard	5	15	100		Battleline in an **YMETRICA** army
Vanari Auralan Sentinels	10	20	140		See notes for Vanari Auralan Wardens
Vanari Dawnriders	5	20	130		See notes for Vanari Auralan Wardens
Alarith Temple	-	-	120	Warscroll Battalion	
Auralan Legion	-	-	120	Warscroll Battalion	
Dawnrider Lance	-	-	120	Warscroll Battalion	
Teclian Vanguard	-	-	80	Warscroll Battalion	
Hyshian Twinstones	1	1	30	Endless Spell	
Rune of Petrification	1	1	70	Endless Spell	
Sanctum of Amyntok	1	1	30	Endless Spell	

FACTION	ALLIES
Lumineth Realm-lords	Idoneth Deepkin